EVERLAS ̶ ̶ ̶ ̶ GREEN

Published by
KINGS OF LUIGHNE PUBLISHING
10803 Adare Drive Fairfax VA 22032

Hara, Edward 1949 -
Everlasting Green /Edward Hara

Kings Of Luighne Publishing

ISBN-13: 978-0615811895

ISBN-10: 0615811892

To Someone who has become a wonderful friend and defender of the faith! I hope you enjoy my stories

These stories are dedicated to my friend, Sandra Latsha, who taught me much about grace under suffering by her shining example of patience and courage.

Sandra Sue Latsha
January 21, 1946 – June 17, 2011.

Eternal rest grant unto her, O Lord, and let perpetual light shine upon her. May the souls of the faithful departed, through the mercy of God, rest in peace. Amen.

Grant to your servant, Sandy, O Lord, blessed repose
&
eternal memory.

TABLE OF CONTENTS

Short Stories

Everlasting Green   Page 1

A House Full of Cats   Page 10

Petey, Petey, Parakeety   Page 16

The Butterfly Dancers   Page 33

The Song of the Saw-whet Owl   Page 41

A Pony for Ray   Page 49

The Most Beautiful Place in the World   Page 59

Dirty Old Dog   Page 84

Bobby, Torrington Bulldog   Page 98

Mu'izz   Page 106

Flat Bottom Billy   Page 121

True Hearts of the Sawtooth Range   Page 139

Sacrament   Page 154

Poems

I Hear You, Thomas Merton   Page 168

Musings of a Potential Monk   Page 169

*All photographs and drawings used in this book are taken from public domain files.

EVERLASTING GREEN

Jack Flanders sat on his front steps staring at the last bit of sunlight playing across a pale blue sky. His eyes scanned the field across the road from his house, lingering on each detail of late summer flowers, colored Fall leaves, and the skyline beyond a copse of trees. Beyond that, where sky met horizon, rolling hills reached up to touch the deep purple clouds of a dying day. Golden rays cast glorious beams across a pale blue sky. Behind him, the firm wooden slap of the screen door closing announced the arrival of his son.

"Brought ya some coffee, dad,"

Jack took the cup wordlessly, a nod of his head the only thanks he would offer. His son, Russell, knew from years of experience this was his father's way. It puzzled him why his father couldn't give a simple expression of gratitude, but he had long since let it go. A few years of counseling had helped to somewhat understand his father. After all, if he was going to live with him and take care of his last days, he had better learn how to deal with their differences.

"Kinda warm tonight, ain't it?" he said settling in next to the old man.

Jack merely nodded at his son and gave an affirmative grunt. Russell watched him slowly lift the steaming mug to his lips, pausing long enough to test how hot it was, then take a tentative sip. That was followed by a longer sip, held in the mouth for several seconds to savor the flavor before finding its way down his throat.

"Coffee's good."

There was a long silence between them. Russell watched the sky slowly dim. All around him a chorus of a thousand insects called to one another, a great harmonious melody of sounds, high and low, short and long, bidding the day farewell.

"Where are you, Dad?"

"What do you mean?"

"I mean you've been coming out here every night for the last couple of weeks. You sit here and get this faraway look in your eyes while you watch the sun go down. Are you on a golf course somewhere? Back in World War II on the deck of the U.S.S. Raleigh? Are you watching the sun go down over the Pacific Ocean and wishing you were there again? Where are you, Dad?"

His father turned toward him with a soft smile. There was an unusual look of tenderness in his eyes, and it came through his voice as he replied.

"I'm sorry you weren't raised in the South, son." His voice was low and almost apologetic. Jack closed his eyes and took in a deep, slow breath, savoring the sounds and smells of dusk draping its gentle cloak over the landscape.

"When I was a pup, we would spend the whole day in woods so thick you would think you were lost, except that you knew that old man Porterfield's house was right over the next ridge. You never learned what it is to swing on a muscadine vine and drop into a cool creek on a hot summer day. To climb a hundred foot tall loblolly pine, lock your feet around the branches and swing in the wind." He leaned back and stretched, then let out a long chuckle. "If your grandma had ever caught me doing that she woulda had a canary. She was always frettin' over us."

Another long breath. Russell could see that Dad was far away in another time, another place. "And after a whole day of living, just being alive in the best way you could, I would come home, have one of your grandma's good dinners. And when the sun started to set, I would go sit on our porch and listen to the cicadas and the katydids saying goodnight to the day. I always loved hearing that at the end of the day.

"Where'm I at, boy? I'm sitting on yer grandma's porch." Jack rested his head in his hand, his cheek against the palm. His voice was wistful and full of memory.

"You know, when you're a young boy, the whole world's a wonderful place because you haven't grown up, and you haven't experienced its pain yet. To me, the best thing in the world was to go out at night at the end of a perfect day and to listen to the cicadas sing to each other. The whole chorus of nature would sing me to sleep at night.

You wanna know where I'm at? I'm back home. I'm sorry you never learned to walk into a forest of nothing but pine trees – beautiful loblolly pine trees – where the whole floor of the forest is carpeted with pine straw. You never learned the joy of laying down with your face in the pine straw and smelling the beautiful smell of that brown pine straw and everything being so perfect because you were born in the South and the South will always be your home. All you ever got from me as a kid was that nasty concrete jungle called Baltimore.

You hear bugs singing. I hear the South calling me home. I come out here, remember a little bit, and wish I was back there – back home." He turned up his cup, draining down the last of the coffee, then carefully placed it on the concrete between them. "Guess I'm just spending time wishing I was young and the world was joy again."

Russell stared at his father in amazement. It was the most he had heard from him in months. He hadn't expected this depth of his father's soul offered to him. Lacking any response, he picked up the coffee cup between them and stood up and turned to the door to go inside. He paused with his hand on the handle of the old wooden screen door.

"That's nice, Dad." A pause. No response. "I'll warm this up for ya" Russell disappeared into the house, the song of the cicadas still singing in his ears. He returned, sat beside his father, and held the cup out to him.

"Here ya go."

The old man was still. He was still for a long time.

"Dad?" He reached out and put a hand on his father's shoulder. The simple touch caused the body to roll to one side. Russell quickly grabbed him, releasing the cup to shatter all over the porch. He fiercely drew his father to him, clutching him as if to try to keep the last of the life in him, and crying out in sorrow.

❀❀❀❀❀

Funerals are such messy things. You can't even bury the dead in peace anymore. There's paperwork and paperwork and when you think that all the paperwork is done, someone comes in from some stupid agency with another paper to sign. Somehow Russell tolerated it all without losing his well known temper until the final insult came in the form of a state probation officer who solemnly told him that he wasn't cleared to get on the plane to Atlanta with his father's body.

"What the hell are you talking about?"

"Don't yell at me, boy." The man's face showed no emotion. "We haven't got a travel voucher on file for you." The voice was cold and factual. "Did you file an emergency travel form?"

Russell glared at him, wanting to punch him in the face. "No one told me I needed one to go bury my Dad."

"Your father should have told you that he was going to be buried in Georgia, not Maryland."

"You're kidding! I didn't even know that until the funeral director told me yesterday."

"That's not my problem, son. And you better unclench those fists. You take a swing at me and I'll have you back in the joint so fast it'll make your head spin." The probation officer lowered his glasses with a finger. "That's after I beat the living crap outta ya, son. So you better cool down" Without another word he turned and walked away, his shoes crunching on the gravel driveway, leaving Russell muttering under his breath about all the things he would like to do to this pompous ass.

Three months later Russell stood outside St. Charles Boromeo parish and stared at the wrinkled white paper he had found while going through his father's possessions. An hour spent in the cemetery had not turned up his dad's grave. Now he wondered if this cryptic note offered him some sort of clue.

Dear Russell –

When you lay me to rest, you will have questions.

Fr. Damon has the answers. Find him.

In a quiet place, where cicadas call, where blue of eternity meets

everlasting green, there I lie with the one you never knew.

Where blue of eternity meets everlasting green? What answers? Russell stared off into the distance. Blue of eternity? Everlasting green? His eyes played over the landscape. Before him lay a flat carpet of grass, dotted with the random tombstones of the old cemetery. Beyond the pointed spires of the wrought iron fence, the land disappeared into the distance. To his right stood a majestic grove of pines, the only color against the drab hues of oncoming winter.

"Boy, Dad would have loved this," he mused. As if in agreement, one of the pines swayed slightly in the wind. Russell watched the green boughs waving gently in the breeze, wondering where the priest might be.

Green. Evergreen! Those are evergreens. He looked at the paper again. *Where the blue of eternity meets the everlasting green.* The blue sky framed the waving green boughs. Russell shook his head and snorted. "Way to go, Dad. Always the mystery about you." He slowly walked toward the grove, his hands folding the note and putting it back in his pocket.

Even though the sun was high in the noon day sky, the grove was dim and somewhat mysterious looking. The numerous branches shut out most of the sunlight. Russell entered slowly, letting his eyes adjust to the dim light. He had walked perhaps twenty feet when he saw the graves. One looked new. The other was covered with pine straw, the stone was chipped and tilted with age. The new grave was his father's.

"I suppose you would be Jack's son." The voice was soft and friendly. Russell turned around to see a priest standing to his right behind him. The priest stuck out his right hand. "I'm Father Damon."

"Who's this?" Russell asked, pointing to the other grave.

"You don't know?" The priest looked stunned. "Your Dad never told you?" There was a long silence, followed by a deep sigh. He took a few steps over to the grave and knelt beside it, making the sign of the cross. "This is your brother, George. As you see, he died a long time ago when he was very young." Father Damon fixed his eyes on Russell. "You don't know anything about this, do you?"

Russell shook his head.

Father Damon continued in a low voice. "Your Mom and Dad were on vacation. They turned their back on him for a second and he was gone. His body was found months later but they never found out who killed him. Or why."

Father Damon rose and turned to Russell. Russell could see emotion in the priest's face as he continued. "It killed your father. He blamed himself, but more than that, he blamed God. He never forgave himself and he lost his faith. Your mother was stronger and she worked through it, but your father never forgave God for letting it happen."

Russell took a deep breath and let it out slowly. "Wow." He shook his head from side to side. "That explains a lot. I don't think I ever saw my Dad laugh when I was a kid. I always blamed myself that he was unhappy. I always thought it was my fault. It took me years of counseling in prison to understand that it wasn't my fault he was unhappy, but I never knew why he was so miserable – until today." He gave Father Damon a puzzled look. "You said that he lost his faith, yet he came to you to be buried?"

"Are you Catholic, Russell?"

"Sort of. I guess. I mean, church is okay on Christmas and Easter, but I don't go much other than then."

"Do you know what it means to make a good confession?"

Russell nodded.

"When Jack found out he was dying he called me. We've been friends longer than dirt has been around. He was pretty embarrassed to come to me after moving away and ignoring my letters, but I told him better late than never. We talked a lot, and then about two months ago he shows up on my doorstep one day wanting to talk. Flew down here just to see me. We talked for a long time, then he made confession." Father Damon's head slowly nodded up and down. "He made a real good confession."

The old priest put his hand on Russell's shoulder. "He asked me to tell you he's sorry he wasn't a better father to you. When we were talking, he told me that he had come to see how selfish he had been and how he had hurt you." There was a pause as Father Damon weighed his words. "I knew your Dad real well. He couldn't express affection. He was afraid to let himself love you. He was so scared of the pain he had gone through when George died."

"Scared? My Dad?" Russell snorted and shook his head. "No. One thing I always admired about him was his strength."

"He wasn't strong, Russell. He was a weak and scared man who was fighting terrible fear. He got lost in his sorrow, and unfortunately for you, he never came out of it." Father Damon looked directly into Russell's eyes. "People show the world a lot of things. But priests get to see the real person behind the mask. The sad part is that you got the worst of it." The old priest put his hand on Russell's arm. "He loved you, Russell. He asked me to tell you that." He turned and began to walk out of the grove. "I'll be in my parish office if you want to talk to me later."

Russell turned back to the graves, his hand fishing in his pocket. He dug out the scrap of paper that had accompanied him since he found it.

"Whenever you come to visit me, stretch out on the ground and let the sweet smell of the South comfort you, my son."

My son. A tear worked its way out of one eye. My son. Slowly he released his knees and let himself sink to the ground. Leaning forward, he stretched out over the soft carpet, feeling pine needles scratch through his shirt. He buried his face in the ground and inhaled the rich smell of earth, pine straw, and all that was sacred to that spot.

Above him, pine trees swayed in a soft Georgia breeze.

A HOUSE FULL OF CATS

> 17th Place Honorable Mention
> – Writer's Digest 80th Annual
> Writing Competition
> Inspirational/Spirituality
> Category

There is a small house, nestled in the woods north of Harrisburg. From the back window you can watch deer eat the corn that the woman has her downstairs tenant put out for them. Occasional turkeys come for the feast and one time the woman saw a bear. It was a small brown bear, not much more than a cub.

The house is full of cats, or at least, as full as it should be for a house that size. There is Molly, who is a black-and-white, and Little Boy, who is an orange striped tabby. Beauty is a Maine Coon, with the soft, fluffy fur of that breed. Dinah is a Calico and the grand old lady of the house at twenty-one, which is quite old for a cat. She can be very fussy, the way old ladies – and old men, too – sometimes will be.

The woman lies on her bed. Molly, Dinah, and Little Boy take turns lying on her. Mostly they lie on her lap, although occasionally you can find one of them lying on the woman's lap and one lying on her chest a the same time.

Molly is the hardest of the cats for the woman to tolerate, for Molly is plump and well fed , which makes her heavier than the other two who take turns lying on her. But she loves Molly and lets Molly lie on her chest anyway, even though it is uncomfortable.

There are four other cats who share the house along with these four, and even some feral cats outside the house, who are fed by the aides who come to care for the woman. The other cats inside the house are not as friendly as Molly, Little Boy, Beauty, and Dinah, so you hardly see them. If you enter the living room, they will run and hide under chairs and couches. The feral cats will come up on the deck to eat the food put out for them, but at the first noise they will scatter and head back into the woods. There was once a mother cat with five kittens, but no one has seen her or the kittens for over a year and the woman worries that perhaps they got hit by a car, or picked up and sent to an animal shelter. She is afraid that they might have been put to sleep. She talks about them and worries about them because she loves animals.

The woman is in her early 60's. She lies on her bed most of the time. She does so because MS took her legs from her, then her arms, and now all she can move is her head. She has attendants come to stay with her around the clock. And the cats. They stay around the bed, they sleep with her, and they are her comfort. When she has to go to the hospital she misses them terribly, and worries whether they are being properly cared for in her absence.

There is a man who comes to visit from time to time. Sometimes he comes over because he wants to and sometimes he comes because she calls him when her aides cannot get to the house. When the man comes to see her, Molly is the first to greet him. Molly didn't let the man touch her the first few times he came. Now she comes right up to him and jumps in his lap, much to his delight, because he likes cats and likes to scratch Molly under her chin. Molly purrs and nestles into his lap.

Then Beauty, hearing the purring, will come out from hiding and meow at the man. She makes little circles in front of the man until he puts his hand down and she rubs her face against his hand. He knows he can't pick her up because she is fearful of people. It took a long time for the man to become her friend. It is because her right hind leg was caught in a trap. Half of the paw is missing and she is still scared. But that is okay with the man. Perhaps some day she will let him pick her up.

The woman is the man's friend. He came to know her one day a few years ago when a mutual friend invited the man over to her house. Overtime he has gotten to know her better and now he cares about her a lot. That is why he comes over just to visit. He brings her sandwiches, and clam chowder, which she loves. He patiently feeds her because her arms cannot move and she cannot feed herself. She smiles at the man and says *"thank you"* to him for bringing her the food she likes but cannot get most of the time. The man smiles back at her and tells her that he is happy to do it for her. Then, when he is done, he gets up to wash the dishes and feed the cats if they need to be fed.

"Perhaps if I gave Beauty a little tuna from my hand...." the man thinks, wondering how he can get her up on his lap so he can fuss over her like he does with Molly. But he doesn't mind because at least she lets him pet her, even if it is not on his lap. The man is happy that he can even touch Beauty because she doesn't let most people near her. The man is not sure whether Beauty or Molly is his favorite, but he is quite fond of Beauty because she is such a beautiful cat with her long, soft Maine Coon fur.

When the man comes to visit the woman, he sometimes thinks of his wife, who died three years ago. His wife was sick like the woman, except that she didn't have MS. She died from a stroke that put her in a bed also, and which took her away from him very slowly. She was in a nursing home which was four hours from where they lived. The man never saw her very much, and after she died – many months after she died – he began to regret that he had not sacrificed more of his time to drive to Pittsburgh and be with his wife.

A year after his wife died the man left his home and went away. He was seeking answers and some peace in his heart. He went to a monastery and prayed and worked and ate with the monks. He fell in love with the life of the monastic order and he thought surely he would become a monk. But God came to him one night in a way he wasn't expecting and showed him that he should go back home and learn to love people. The man was brought to understand very clearly how he had only thought of himself all his life and how he had never really learned what love is because love is not thinking romantic thoughts about others. Love is doing and serving and sacrifice for others, which the man suddenly knew in his heart he had never done. The man spent the night crying and praying, and the next day packed his bags, said goodbye to the monks, and drove back home. He went back to work during the day and at night he read books and thought about what God had shown him. He wondered and prayed about how to show love to the people in his life. Then, one day, a few months after he had returned from the monastery, the woman called him.

"I'm sorry to bother you," she said, *"but none of my aides can come today and I don't want to be alone. I hate to ask you, but could you come over to sit with me for a while?"*

The man thought about it for a few seconds, and as he thought, he remembered what God had sent him home to do and he said *"yes"*.

He went over to her house. Molly ignored him, Beauty wouldn't let him touch her, and the time seemed to drag on forever. Then he went home, said his prayers, and sat on the edge of his bed thinking.

"I suppose this is love," he thought, *"because I am doing something to help her. And it is sacrifice because I really didn't want to go over there and help her, but I did it because it was the right thing to do."* But he was puzzled to think of it as love because he associated love with feelings and it simply didn't *feel* like love to him.

She called again a week later. And again, and two weeks after that, because for some reason, all of a sudden she was having a terrible time getting aides to come to take care of her. Every time she called, she apologized. And every time the man told her not to apologize and that he didn't mind coming over, even though sometimes he did. He wished he could feel more loving about it, but nonetheless, he realized that it was the right thing to do, regardless of how he felt, so he did it.

Then one night she called and asked if he could stay with her all night.

"I'll try," he said, letting a sigh slip out of the side of his mouth so that it would not go through the phone and the woman would not hear it, *"but I may fall asleep because I am not used to staying up all night. I just want you to know that and be ready for it."*

"I don't care," she told him, *"as long as you are here and I am not alone."*

So he went over and spent the night. He did fall asleep sitting in the chair next to her bed and she didn't care because he was there with her.

When she had to return to the hospital a few weeks later he went to visit her there because he thought she must be lonely and he couldn't imagine how boring it must be to just lie around and have no one to talk to.

One day, in her hospital room the subject of hospital food came up. She mentioned how nice it would be to have some decent food like Coconut Shrimp from Outback Steak House, which was her favorite. So a few days later he went to the restaurant and then to the hospital. She was happy and smiled at the man, and as he sat there and fed her Coconut Shrimp from Outback Steak House, he realized that his heart was full of joy.

Two weeks later the woman was better and she returned to the house full of cats. They were all very happy to see her. The man came over to visit and she told him how happy she was to be back home with her cats. Molly lay on her chest and Little Boy snuggled in her lap and the man scratched Beauty on the head while they talked, for Beauty still would not let him pick her up.

One night she called again and the man went over to be with her so she wouldn't be alone. So many things go wrong with the body when a person cannot move. The woman has problems with her eyes. They water and the tears run down her cheeks, which is very annoying to her. She asked the man to take a tissue and wipe her eyes. He gently lifted her glasses up, took a tissue, and began to wipe the tears away – something he had done many times before.

"Is that okay?" he asked, his voice soft with concern for her comfort.

"That's fine. Thank you." Then she seemed to settle in, closed her eyes, and was very quickly asleep, which was fine with the man, for he didn't wish her to see him as he wiped the tears from the corners of his eyes.

If you can find the house full of cats, which is near the woods north of Harrisburg – if you know where to go – and you drop in for a visit, you may meet the man. He prays for her every day and he tries to go over there once or twice a week, even when she doesn't call. And if you do find him there, he will be sitting with Beauty on his lap, and Molly and Little Boy will be lying on the woman in their usual places.

PETEY, PETEY, PARAKEETY

The first time I saw Petey was when I met his owner, Bryce Clawson, I was making my rounds at Sunny Valley Nursing Home. I came to Room 114 and noticed new name on the door where Mrs. Johnston had been, so I knocked on the door and waited for a reply. I don't like to go barging in on people's privacy, even if I have known them for a while.

There was a gruff grunt from inside, which I took to be some sort of approval to come in. I took a few steps inside the room and saw Bryce lying on the bed. A parakeet, bright green with a white head, was balanced on his finger, close to Bryce's left shoulder.

"Beat it!" The voice was sharp and unfriendly. The bird jumped and fluffed his feathers, apparently startled by the loud reaction. "Go on, get out!"

A priest never intrudes upon the wishes of others, even if you want to do good for them, like praying with them, so I turned to leave.

"And don't come back!" It was a loud shout, almost a roar. It must have scared the little bird because the next thing I knew, he was sitting on my shoulder. I put slowly put my finger up to him and he stepped up on it ever so politely.

"Petey, come here! Get away from that nasty priest!" The voice lowered to a pleading tone. "Come here, Petey. Come to Pappa."

I turned to face Bryce and moved my hand toward the bed, but the bird didn't leave my finger. I was unsure what to do at first, then I decided that despite this man's obvious dislike for me, I would do the charitable thing. I walked slowly up to the bed and extended my finger to the old guy. He glared at me for a second, then put his finger next to mine until Petey hopped onto it.

I guess it was foolish to expect thanks. After about a half a minute of his unresponsive silence, I simply nodded my head and walked out of the room. As I did, I heard him scolding his pet, talking to Petey as a mother would a naughty child whom she loves dearly. The tone was unmistakable. That little bird was his whole life.

I stopped by the nurse's desk on my way out. "What's the story on the gentleman in 114?" I asked Linda, the charge nurse on duty. She's a member of my parish and someone I go to frequently for information on patients.

At the word "gentleman" Linda rolled her eyes "Oh, you mean Mr. Personality?" She made the Sign of the Cross and sighed. "He's dying and he's none too happy about it. Takes it out on all of us."

"And our Lord calls you to love him, just as he is. Nasty and all." I laid my hand over hers and in my best encouraging voice continued. "You're a good Catholic, Linda. God has called you to show him the love of Christ. I'll be praying for you."

"Thanks, Father. You know that we pray for you, too."

"I'm surprised you allow a bird in here."

"Birds. Dogs. Cats. All the same. People are dying on this floor, Father.

We don't think it's gonna do something horrible to allow them their last few months with their pets." She gave me that smile of hers that could melt a stone and laughed. "What's gonna happen? You think their pets might give them a fatal disease or something?"

Nothing changed for the next few months. I would walk by Mr. Clawson's room and deliberately look at him and wave. He, in turn, would reward me with some form of gesture or verbal insult intended to make his dislike of priests known to me. Guess he didn't want me to forget how delighted he would be if all priests in the world dropped off the face of the earth.

Petey changed that for us one day.

A new resident moved into the room near the end of the hall. She had a big yellow tabby cat which she claimed was housebroken, but in fact, had a particularly wild streak to it. My first meeting with the cat was to be memorable.

I was at Sunny Valley for my usual Monday afternoon visitation. I had just come to the nurses desk on Bryce Clawson's floor when I heard a shriek and the sound of something metal hitting the floor. I knew the sound of Clawson's voice and took off sprinting for his door. As I got there, all hell broke loose – right on top of me. The yellow tabby leaped and caught the escaping Petey by the tail feathers and they both crashed into my waist below my belt buckle. I made a grab for Petey and somehow my hands found the cat's mouth. I jammed a finger inside to try to loosen the frightened bird. The next instant I cried out in pain as rows of sharp teeth punctured my finger. Mr. Cat was not letting go of his prize without a fight. Petey wiggled free and fell to the floor with a thump. I grabbed the cat by the scruff of the neck and turned to the desk, watching my feet so that I didn't step on Petey.

"Whose cat is this?" I demanded loudly.

"Don't you hurt my Charlie!"

I turned toward the horrified voice screaming at me. A large woman in a nightgown was waddling up the floor as fast as she could, an angry look on her face. She was headed right for Petey, but her scowling gaze was riveted on her cat. Petey was walking between us, apparently in a bit of a daze, and I could just see her stepping on him in her haste to get to Charlie. To make matters worse, Charlie was flailing about, hissing, spitting and scratching whatever parts of my arm and hand he could lay his claws into. This was not good.

In retrospect, I probably could have handled the situation better, but in the stress of the moment, the only thing I could think to do was lower Charlie to the floor and sling him down the hall towards his owner. I was probably pretty pumped up from him ripping into me and sailed him right past her on the waxed floor. He bounced against the far wall near her room. That stopped the woman dead in her tracks, shrieking about how dare I treat her precious feline that way. While she was shrieking, I made a move to catch Petey. He was already freaked out and this just spooked him worse. He took off flying again – right towards the hungry pussums who had gotten up and was charging my way again, his eyes glued on Petey.

It must have looked hilarious to anyone watching. Me chasing the bird with outstretched hands, the woman cursing at me in her nightgown, and Charlie up again and running full steam toward us. As Petey flew overhead Charlie took a leaping swipe at him and missed. Petey hit the far wall and fell like a stone. Charlie skidded on his butt across the floor, got up, and started to run back towards Petey. His legs were moving like Fred Flintstone starting his car – all motion and no traction to speak of. I shot ahead of him and was on Petey immediately, cupping my hands protectively over him. A second later Charlie leaped on my closed hands and dug his claws in – hard!

Without thinking I jumped up and yelled the first thing that came to my mind, the stupid cat still clinging to me with his claws dug deeply into my hands.

"You sorry son-of-a-bitch! GET - OFF - ME!"

I reflexively corkscrewed my body, then unwound sharply, letting the momentum fling Charlie off me and down the hall. When he got up, I growled at him as loud as I could and stamped my feet menacingly. He thought about it a second, then scurried into his room, followed by his still upset momma, who was cussing me out like a sailor. When I turned to look up the hall, there were three nurses staring at me, their mouths in various states of open surprise.

I out a loud sigh and said, "Well, this is embarrassing." It was the only thing I could think to say. Linda cocked her head and then began to laugh uproariously. The other two joined in.

"We'll see you at Confession, Father!" she sang out, still laughing. People forget that priests are human, sometimes more human than we care to be. We don't like our sins to be so public. I shrugged my shoulders, rolled my eyes, and started walking towards Clawson's room, cupping the bird close to my chest. I was hoping he wasn't dead, then I felt him move about a bit. I was smiling when I approached his bed.

"Petey! You have Petey?" His voice was fraught with worry as he stretched his thin arms out toward me. "Gimme. Gimme Petey! Is he okay?" He was shaking with concern for his little friend.

"How about I call a vet and have him come take a look at him?"

"No, no." His voice was still shaking with emotion. "Let's see you, Petey." He held his finger out to the little bird. "Come here. Come on, Petey," he intoned softly. At first Petey wasn't in a big hurry to move. He was probably still freaked out from the whole incident. Then he slowly looked out from my cupped hands and then stepped up onto Clawson's outstretched finger as the old man continued to speak softly to him. Keeping his eyes on the bird, he began to sing quietly.

"Petey, Petey, parakeety. Who's your Pappa's little sweetie?" The little bird moved about and began to preen his feathers. He suddenly seemed oddly calm after his near fatal encounter with the cat. Clawson brought his free hand slowly to the bird and gently stroked the feathers on its back. Then he moved to the front, scratching the feathers on the chest while continuing to sing his little ditty.

"I'm glad he's okay, Mr. Clawson." There was no answer, so I turned to go. I had taken a few steps when I heard Clawson call to me.

"Hey, Mr. Priest. Petey seems to like you. Would you do me a favor and put him in his cage? I think he's had all the excitement he needs for one day." He slowly held his hand out to me and I let Petey climb onto my finger. As I was putting Petey inside for the day, Clawson started to cackle behind me.

"Son-of-a -bitch? You actually called that damned cat a son-of-a-bitch?"

I wonder if I was red with embarrassment when I turned around. Clawson just kept laughing. I suppose the idea of a priest using such coarse language was amusing him to no end. While it was good to see that he could laugh, I was thoroughly embarrassed to have my failures made so public. The fact is, I had been a priest for five years and I couldn't honestly say that I was living the holiest life I could. Now it was really public, and I was none to happy about it. I wondered how many people Linda would tell.

The old guy loosened up with me after our little adventure. Maybe seeing my priestly failings put me in a new light. It was kind of strange. Linda told me he still wouldn't talk to anyone and didn't want any visitors – except me. She was laughing so hard she had to gasp for air as she told me about the Baptist minister he told "go straight to hell and take your Baptist religion with you." Apparently Bryce told him so firmly that the whole floor heard it.

I came to see him three days after I had saved Petey from being a light snack. Bryce must have seen my black suit and collar before he saw my face because the first thing that was out of his mouth before our eyes met was "Beat it!" Then he stared me right in the face and almost seemed a bit embarrassed that he had spoken to me that way after making friends just a couple of days before.

"Sorry," he mumbled. "Didn't know it was you." A pause. "Come on in and pull up a chair."

I pulled up a chair and sat by his bed. At first there was a lot of silence. Bryce wasn't the talking and visiting kind. I tried to make a little chit-chat with him, talking about the weather and such. It was pretty uncomfortable for me, too. I'm used to having people just open up and share the darkest parts of their lives with me. I don't usually have to pry.

Finally I asked him if he was married. That got him started – and good! His wife had cheated on him and then left him for some young guy twenty years his age. She left him with five kids to raise. No one from his parish had come to help him or visit. The priest never came to his house and when one of his children died, he couldn't find the money to pay for a decent burial for the child.

The more I kept quiet and let him talk, the more he went on. He was a man who had been stewing in bitterness for years. He was well-marinated by now, and it was time to share the feast with the whole world before he died. He wanted to let it all out – not in order to repent or set things right, but just to let everyone know just how deeply he hated the world and God. There were days it was just plain old hard to listen to him berate God and cuss out the Church for what he considered all Her failings. He was a lapsed Catholic who was picking a serious – although totally unwarranted – bone with God. I began to hope I could remove that bone before he died.

I don't know why I did it, but one day when we were talking I decided to open up and tell him about my life. I let him know about my leaving the Church, rejecting all that my parents had so diligently tried to instill in me. I told him frankly about my past pornography use, my nights with drugs and women, and some of the more memorable hangovers I had suffered through. He was pop-eyed by the time I finished. And dead silent for along time.

"Well, ain't that something, Mr. Priest." He sucked on a tooth, making a popping noise with his tongue. "I'da never guessed that about you in a million years. You're quite a fella." He was grinning from ear to ear at this unexpected revelation. It seemed to please him to no end to hear about the seamy side of my former life.

"I'm not proud of it, old man." I tried to grin back at him, but I don't think I pulled it off. The pain of the memories I had dredged up was a real ache at that moment.

"Yeah, but you know what? At least you're honest. You're a true human being, not like some of those white plaster statues who drone on in the pulpit and don't know what real life is all about." He nodded his head at me. His eyes took on a more serious look. "I can respect you, Father. Respect you because you've been down the road. They haven't. And they don't know their ass from third base when it comes to real life and giving any kind of worthwhile help to a guy. All I ever got from any of them was nice words that didn't mean a hill of spit."

He inched himself up a little on his bed. "Tell you something else, Mr. Priest. I think you're a real man, too." When I cocked my head to one side, he went on. "I see how you look at that pretty nurse Linda when she comes in the room. You're not fooling me one bit. You may be fooling God with this priest routine, but you ain't fooling me." He chuckled a little bit, very satisfied with pining me down so well.

He irritated me when he said that. Irritated me because down deep in my heart I knew what he was saying was the truth. Seeing Linda somehow played havoc with my emotions. I would get thoughts about her I didn't want to have. I didn't like knowing he could read me so well, and it bothered me to wonder if the other nurses on the floor could see my attraction to Linda as well. I would always go to her first and spent a lot of time talking with her, and that not always about patients. I hope I didn't stare at her the way that Bryce inferred. I could imagine them talking between themselves.

"It's not a routine, Mr. Clawson." My voice had an edge. "Yes, Linda is a pretty lady, but I've made my choice. Am I a man? Yes. Is she a good looking lady? You're darn right she is. But I choose to follow Christ, and that involves me accepting that sacrifice. And sacrifice involves a certain amount of suffering. I make the choice to do this. I make the choice to accept the sacrifice of living a celibate life, just like you make the choice to be angry at God and the world."

I really should have shut up then, but my pride was wounded. The old man had seen right through the facade, and I didn't like it one bit. Now I was on the offensive, and he was going to get both barrels.

"You want to know something? You're not the only person who has ever been mistreated by life. I hear it all – all the sordid details about spouses cheating, friends stealing from friends, and things you just wouldn't believe people do to each other." I paused for effect, then continued on.

"But you know what I find the most inspiring thing about my job?" I leaned in to emphasize my point, looking him right in the eyes. "It's when people tell me they have really forgiven the one who hurt them. It's seeing them move on with their lives and not be bitter. That's what makes my work satisfying."

I was in lecture mode and I kept going.

"You know how monkeys are trapped over in Asia? They put a peanut in a coconut they have fastened to the ground and wait for the monkey to come and stick his hand in the coconut to get the peanut. The monkey won't let go of his treasure and even when he sees the men coming for him, he keeps clinging to the peanut instead of letting go. You're the monkey, all the anger you have against God is the peanut, and you can see the devil coming for you and you still won't give it up. Only God knows why you won't let go, but it's going to wind up trapping you for all eternity.

God loves you, just like He loves everyone on this sad little sin-cursed planet. When you pass from this life to the next, you will see Him in all that love, but you will be so trapped in your bitterness in the next life that you won't be able to return His love. In fact, you won't even understand His love because it will feel like darkness and pain to you. That is what we call hell. Being locked in selfishness and bitterness for all eternity because God wouldn't perform for you like some sort of trained monkey you could command to your every whim in this life.

You know what? It doesn't work that way. It never has. He is God and we aren't. You just couldn't accept that He would allow such pain into your life, but instead of seeking a way to use your pain and become a better person, you have let it turn you into a sour old codger no one wants to be with."

I stood up and turned away from his bed. "You heard my story. I could be angry at God, too. Angry I can't ask Linda out for a date. But I choose not to be." I was speaking in anger, which is never a good thing to do, but even more so as a priest.

"You want to be alone? Fine. God will honor that request – for all eternity! The choice is yours."

I strode out the door quickly, went all the way down the hall to the patient's sunroom, which was empty, and found a corner where I lowered my head and let the tears come out quietly. Everything I had struggled with since my ordination was popping to the surface. How could I give such good advice that I hadn't really followed myself? What was a failure like me doing giving old Clawson any advice? I sat there and let all the doubts come out where I could struggle with them in the silence of my thoughts.

After five years of being a priest, I was really struggling with confusion about my decision to pursue ordination. What had started out as a happy day of congratulations from my parish and joy from my family had come to this: I didn't have any enthusiasm for the things a priest should love to do. Hearing confessions was a chore, I found little joy in celebrating the Mass, and I couldn't stop thinking about Linda.

I let the tears and frustration out for a while, then cleaned myself up and left. Thankfully, no one had walked into the room while I was letting my emotions out. No sense in having to deflect unwanted questions.

Fr. Freddie Morrison is my friend from Smitheville in the next county. We've always been very open with each other about our faults. A couple of days after my encounter with Bryce, I went to visit him. We hugged warmly, as only brothers in the priesthood can do in their shared knowledge of the trials and joys of the priesthood.

"It's good to see you again, John. It's been a while."

"Thanks. Will you hear my confession and then we talk for a bit?"

He arched an eyebrow at me, then nodded toward his church and led the way inside the massive front doors of the old parish. I walked slowly behind him, taking the time to take in all the things I had come to love about this parish, an ancient old church, built in the grey stone style of ancient Gothic cathedrals. It is easily over a hundred years old, although I had never asked and found out just how old. There was something about this building that always made me feel good when I would see it, unlike the low slung, square gymnasium-box of St. Leo's where I was pastor.

I was halfway through the sins I had planned to confess when Freddie stopped me.

"John, why are you doing this to yourself? This is trivia – some of it I doubt I would even classify as sin." He stared at me for a few seconds with a look of real concern in his eyes before continuing. "John, have you ever considered maybe you have a problem with scrupulosity?" I shook my head in denial. Freddie wasn't impressed. He pushed on. It was my turn to get a lecture.

"Don't shake your head. You need to think real long about what I just said." He leaned back, pausing to let me ponder his words, then went on. "I'll tell you something else. Something I've felt since we were classmates back at Mount St. Mary's. I think you've got a problem trusting God. I've been praying for you, John, and hoping you would recognize it and work on it, but I don't see any change from your seminary days." He looked a bit uncomfortable.

"I really owe you an apology. I saw this way back in seminary, but I was too much of a coward to talk to you about it. In retrospect, it probably would have been the right thing to do." He sighed. "Maybe it would have kept you from what you are going through now."

I didn't have anything to say. I couldn't. He was right. Deep inside I knew that he was right. Why did I become a priest anyway? Was it to make my parents proud of me? They were so happy when I returned to the faith. I knew I had hurt them deeply with my years of chasing my disordered passions. Was it to pay them back for the pain I had caused them?

Or was it to fulfill a promise to the people at St. Anselm's, who used to tell me what a fine priest I would make? I would look at the sisters who were encouraging me and promise that I would consider becoming a priest. Had I felt that I owed them something for promises made while still just young kid?

Perhaps Freddie was right about being scrupulous. Could it be that I really haven't fully accepted that God has forgiven me; that my going to the seminary was trying to somehow to please Him out of a misplaced sense of guilt? I spent four years running from God and directly to a life of sin in which I left no stone unturned. It was as if I had been determined to get as far away from the Catholic faith as possible. Was going to seminary a kind of self-imposed penance after I returned contritely to St. Anselm's and went to my first confession in a long time? Had I moved too fast when I went to Father Bell and told him that I was thinking about becoming a priest? Maybe he should have discouraged me and told me to consider it for a while longer instead of pushing me towards seminary. Everyone was so happy to hear that I had been accepted to the seminary. No one seemed to think that perhaps I needed a few years to get my feet under me after living in scandal.

I ran all these questions by Freddie, one by one. We talked about my past and the things I had done, and the general guilt I was still carrying over the fact that my pornographic past was still very much alive in me. It felt unconquered and some days, barely controlled.

"I hate it, Freddie. Good Lord, what have I done to myself? My mind is so filled with those images that I can't look at young women anymore without thinking things that would get me slapped if they could read my mind. And the summer's the worst – all those low cut blouses the girls seem to feel they have to wear. Every Sunday when I'm giving out Communion I get a show I don't need and don't want. But the worst part is that I know there's a part of me inside that really enjoys it."

I leaned back on the chair the confessional and sighed. Freddie was looking at me as if searching for his next words. I decided to launch into the story about Petey and Charlie and my awful and public response to Charlie. When I was done Freddie took a deep breath, chortled under his breath, then burst out laughing.

"John, that's the funniest story I've heard in a long time." He snickered as he tried to suppress his laughter, than burst out laughing again. "What a sight that must have been!" He paused to compose himself, then stopped smiling and looked at me with serious intent.

"You know what I hear you saying? You're not upset that you offended God. You're upset because you didn't hold up the image of the holy priest that you are so desperate to maintain in front of people."

"A priest should be holy, Freddie. Don't you believe that? Isn't a priest supposed to set the example to follow? How can my people follow me when I am not leading? How can I get them to be what I am not?"

"You point the way, John. Then you walk the journey *with* them. Nothing says you have to just lead. You can let them know you are going on the same tough road they are. It's a journey we all make, and while we are indeed leaders, we also struggle with that same walk."

"Hogwash, Freddie." I paused to gather my thoughts, then blurted out, "I'm going to quit the priesthood, Freddie. I don't belong."

Freddie didn't seem overly surprised or concerned as he answered me calmly, "That's between you and God. I'm not going to tell you what to do one way or the other. I think you're a good priest, despite the faults you have shared with me. We're all on a journey, John, but who knows, maybe you did take a wrong turn. You have to figure this out for yourself. But whatever you do, I'll always be your friend and any time you need to talk, you just call."

I started crying after he said that. His words were a freedom that burst open a dam of emotions for me. I haven't been able to share my doubts and failures with anyone. I guess I was afraid of in some way disappointing my family and the people in my parish, seeing all the hopes that were pinned on me at my ordination. Something about his response, after I had been so open with him about my failures, touched me deep inside. A man needs friends like that. People who will just accept him with all his failures and blemishes. I wonder if people realize how dreadfully lonely it can be from time to time, being a priest and keeping up the appearance. I was just dog tired of it all.

Two days later I was called out of town to care for another parish on the other side of the state. Alex Dumont caught bad case of the flu and spent a week at St. Joe's hospital in Bayard. Even after he came back to the rectory, I was still needed for another two weeks to keep things running smoothly. My associate was given the opportunity to run St. Leo's in my absence as Bishop Satherwaite ordered me to stay with Alex's parish, over my protests and concern for the patients at Sunny Valley.

When I got back to Sunny Valley, Linda met me at the nursing station before I could go down the hallway.

"Father John, Mr. Clawson's gone." For some reason she came up real close to me and began to riffle through her purse. I could smell the perfume she always seemed to wear. Nice, not to strong, but nice. Her voice was low as she fished through her purse. "You should see this. I think you'd like to see this." She fumbled about some more, then produced a picture. "This is how I found him. No one knows I took this picture." Her eyes let me know she was sharing a secret with me that could get her in a lot of trouble. "I've got to tell you, I was so surprised to find him like this I just had to take this picture for you. I know what he meant to you."

Bryce was lying on the bed. His eyes were closed and he actually looked kind of peaceful. The Rosary I had given him a few months earlier was entwined in the fingers of his right hand, with his thumb and forefinger grasping one of the beads. But the thing that caught my attention the most was in the center of the picture. Petey was lying on Bryce's chest. I looked at Linda questioningly.

"Petey?"

"We found him lying on Mr. Clawson. He was dead." Linda lowered her voice and shook her head gently. "Guess the only two friends they had in the world were each other."

"Come on!" I shook my head in disbelief. "This kind of stuff only happens in sappy novels."

"No, Father. This is real life and it really does happen."

I spent an hour with Bishop Satherwaite. I told him everything I was feeling and every sin I was struggling with. He was understanding. He's placed me on administrative leave to sort things out. I asked to be laicized, but he refused the request.

"You're a good priest, John. And believe it or not, you're not the first priest to ever struggle with these things. Let's give this some time to work itself out between you and God. If you still feel the same way at the end of a year, I'll reconsider your request. But I want you to come talk to me every month and let's see if we can help you figure out what God's will is for your life."

I'll go along with the bishop for now. I have some plans to take some personal time to do some things I have been neglecting, including playing golf, which I am good at but haven't enjoyed for some time.

I don't know what I'm going to do about Linda. She's the monkey wrench in the works. The fact is that she is a near occasion of sin for me and one that I don't need around me, given I am so strongly attracted to her, both as a woman and as a devout Catholic.

I finally decided to take Linda out to dinner. She's been the head of the Altar Guild for five years now and has done a great job. I thought it was past time that she got a little appreciation for the fine work she has done, so I went to the parish council and suggested this dinner as a reward for good service.

They were all for it. Of course, they didn't know the real reason for it, and I wasn't about to tell them. Unless I get a special grace of celibacy that I don't feel now, I don't know what I'm going to do about my feelings and the gnawing interest I have in her. Our dinner was lovely, even with Fr. Canolph with us, and I couldn't stop thinking about how nice it would be to spend the rest of my life with her.

A couple of days after our dinner, I spent an hour on the phone with Freddie. His wise advice was to distance myself from Linda and the parish. In the end, I've decided to move out of the rectory and quietly attend Mass at St.

Vincent's on the other side of town. Hopefully nobody will recognize me there and I can work out my issues without having to see Linda sitting in the pews of St. Leo's every Sunday. I think the distance between us will help me work out my feelings for her as I pray and consider my future.

I have obtained a position with Mayfair Country Club to work at their golf course. I particularly enjoy running the gang-mower over the fairways. The purr of the diesel engine and the cool of the mornings, watching the sun make its ascent as I mow, all that gives me the quiet and time I need to think and pray about all this. It's nice to just sit on the bench at the third tee box and watch the sun come up over the small pond that guards the par three green. I haven't felt this much peace in quite a while, and I am getting to like it.

I'll see what my feelings are about everything after I've had the year off. For now, I'm content to put on my civilian clothes and get in touch with the world again. There was no information given other than a small announcement in the bulletin telling the parish that I was taking time off for a needed rest. That's all they need to know for now.

I'm also going to visit my older brother, Steve, who lives out in Kansas City. He was the only one who had enough sense to seriously question my decision to enter the seminary, and, for that, he became somewhat of a pariah in the family. I think he saw something that everyone else in their excitement failed to observe. I have a feeling that he will be my biggest help in sorting this all out. I've was so busy running St. Leo's that I seem to have lost sense of who I really am and what my life should be. Steve will help me slow down and smell the roses. And when we talk about everything that has transpired over the last couple of years, I know he won't pull any punches either.

I pray every night for old Bryce's soul. I hope it's doing him good.

THE BUTTERFLY DANCERS

Ben Norris had spent a year trying to achieve what he finally accomplished that morning. Every day he came down to Ashton Park to sit on the park bench facing the playground, staring ahead blankly through the haze of his hangover. The park regulars, young women with their infants in brightly-colored strollers, joggers who circled the park, and the businessmen who came for lunch, kept a good distance from him, and rightly so. Ben was mean. He was an ill-tempered, ragged, and unshaven specter of a man, a gaunt and haunted shell of a once reasonably happy life. He knew what he was and he didn't care. If his life was going to be a living hell, then no one else around him should be allowed the luxury of happiness. He would not suffer alone.

Every morning, inquisitive pigeons would slowly approach his bench, warily looking for a meal while watching with the careful fear of man that God has put in wild creatures. For the first few weeks of his self-imposed solitude, Ben let them get close to the bench, then with an awkward, lunging growl sent them exploding off in all directions. He did this everyday, several times a day, until the birds would not approach him anymore.

For the next few weeks after that, he sat alone and grumbled to himself, cursing and waving his hands at the occasional bird that forgot who he was and wandered too close. One day he got the idea of bringing along a bag of bread. He tore the bread to pieces and scattered it around his bench, watching and waiting, taking furtive sips from a hip flask as he looked for his opportunity. When he had drawn the birds in close enough, he would lunge forward trying to catch one of them. Occasionally he would awkwardly attempt to kick one of them from his seat on the bench.

It was on this morning that one of his attempts actually found its mark. The bird was sick and couldn't move fast enough to avoid the foot that sent it tumbling into a trash can. Ben was instantly to his feet, wobbling unsurely as he started for the downed bird. He didn't expect the little girl who seemed to materialize out of nowhere in front of him. He froze and shook his head, not sure of what he was seeing. Where did she come from?

"That was mean," she said in a soft and factual tone. "It makes God sad when you are mean like that." She looked directly into his eyes.

"There is no God!" he started to say with an angry growl, but he got only as far as the word "there" before the rest of the words froze in his throat. The result was an inarticulate grunt which barely escaped his lips. He could only stand and stare at her, his anger against God somehow muffled by her innocent stare.

"My Mommy told me that when I go to heaven I'm gonna be a butterfly." She hadn't even turned to look at the bird that lay still beside the trash can. Her eyes bored into his until he suddenly turned away, stepping back in shock. Except for the blonde hair, she reminded him of Tessie. Reminded him of the daughter that God had ....

Yes, he would say it to himself and the world. The daughter that God had killed. Oh, God didn't actually do the killing, but He had allowed it to happen. God, all powerful and all knowing, yet not caring enough to keep a drug-wasted teenage kid from running a red light, hitting another car, and bouncing across the street to...

He screamed, an incoherent, angry scream from the depths of his soul, trying to chase away the picture of his daughter's crushed body– the horrible memory of her death – bearing in on him. He stumbled forward, seized the back of the park bench and shook it, trying with all his might to rip it apart in his anger.

He raised his face to the heavens and cursed God. "You killed her!" A torrent of curses flowed from his mouth. He pounded on the bench with his fists, then collapsed on it in a miserable heap of dirty, raging sorrow.

After several minutes of sitting, making inarticulate, angry noises, he realized he was no longer alone. A young woman was standing in front of him, staring at him with a mixture of compassion and concern.

"Whaddya want?" he snarled. There was no strength to even push her away. Staring back at her, he could only mumble. "Go 'way."

"I can't," she responded quietly. "I've been watching you for over a month. How you come down here every morning. How you sit here and hate the world and everyone in it." He noticed she was cradling the dead bird in her hands.

"Why?" she asked, slowly offering the bird in his direction. "It's just a pigeon. What would make you be so mean?"

"Whadda you care?"

"I care to see another human being killing himself."

"Oh, God. A do-gooder." He spat the last words out as if they were something bitter in his mouth. "Go way, lady. Leave me alone."

Her eyes seemed to darken a little. She gently set the pigeon on the bench, next to Ben "Here's your pigeon. Enjoy your victory." She turned slowly and walked away. Was that sarcasm in that last statement? No matter. "Up yours, lady." he mumbled under his breath as she slowly disappeared. He looked around. There was no sign of the little girl. He shook his head, then brushed the dead pigeon from the bench, lay down, and was soon asleep.

The young woman was there the next morning, sitting on his bench, waiting for him with a paper cup of hot coffee in a tray. He started to growl at her again, but his thirst for the coffee overrode his desire to be mean to her. He lifted the hot cup to his temple, then moved it slowly to the front of his head, savoring the feel of the heat against his throbbing forehead. After several minutes, the pain subsided considerably. He took a grateful drink and then, despite himself, growled at her.

"What?"

There was kindness and sorrow in her voice. "Whatever it is, you'll never drink the pain away. All you'll wind up doing is killing yourself. Is that what you want?"

There was a very long silence. Finally she rose to go.

"My daughter," he intoned flatly. The woman sat back down.

"She died right over there." The words came slowly and with pain. "She went to get a drink and some stoned kid ran over her with his car."

"Not your daughter." Despite her revulsion at his dirty body, her hand found its way to rest on his forearm. "God's daughter. Our children are only on loan to us." She fumbled in her overly large handbag for a couple of seconds, then produced a picture. "I had to come to understand that when Allie died." She turned the picture toward him and offered it. "It took me a year to get over her death, and the only way I was able to do it was to understand that God has His reasons and we don't own our children. They are on loan to us. We raise them for Him. He trusts us to do a good job and sometimes He simply wishes them to be with Him." She took a long, deep breath, then let it out in a long, resigned sigh. "The pills and the craziness were killing me. I had to let go."

She laughed and it came out as a soft snort through her nose. "You know what she told me one day? She told me that when she died, she wanted to be a butterfly." A pause, another small chuckle. Ben thought he saw a bit of moisture at the corner of her eye. "I told her that God would let her be a butterfly if that was what she wanted."

Ben looked at the picture and stared in shock. It was the little girl from yesterday. There was no mistaking her, from the ringlets of blonde curls spilling down over her shoulders to the unusual birthmark on the right side of her face.

"She died in a car wreck. We never saw the truck coming until it hit us." She looked away. "March fifteenth of last year." A deep sigh. She rose from the bench. "Let me know when you want to talk about your daughter."

Ben watched her disappear in stunned silence, his mind still trying grasp what he had just seen. As she did, a large, yellow Tiger Swallowtail dropped out of the sky, fluttered around the woman's head for a few seconds, then, floating on a soft breeze, landed on a butterfly bush at the side of the park. It went from flower to flower, its wings gently rising and falling. Satisfied, it took to the air and flew directly towards Ben.

There are moments in life when a person is struck with the knowledge that what is happening is beyond human comprehension. To many people, odd events are merely coincidence, but for those who ponder such events, they are far too unbelievable to be just coincidence. A great hand moves people, places, and events to fit a design that we cannot see. Our eyes suddenly open, we see what is happening, and yet it is still unbelievable: the event of the miraculous breaking into our sad little mundane world challenges our disbelief. Emile Zola at Lourdes. The Pharisees watching Jesus raise Lazarus from the dead. There is that moment of suspended rationality, that distortion of life and challenge to our beliefs which calls for a response.

The Swallowtail flew by Ben, then rose straight up in the air. Hovering twenty feet above Ben's head, it played with the wind, dancing back and forth, tumbling through the sunshine. He watched in disbelief, his thoughts raging.

"There is no God, there is no such thing as bread turning into human flesh for our salvation, and children don't die and become butterflies."

Ben slowly lifted his right arm and extended his hand toward the butterfly. For a moment, it continued its airborne dance, then gracefully dropped from the air to settle on the tip of Ben's outstretched finger. Ignoring the sound of his mind screaming to him that he was losing his sanity, he carefully drew his arm back until he held the tip of his finger in front of his face. The butterfly turned on his finger, its proboscis gently probing the skin of Ben's finger.

"This is stupid." he thought. *"Children don't die and become butterflies."*

"Allie? Can you go get Tessie for me?"

"Why are you talking to a butterfly, Mister?" The voice was happy and giggling, laughing at the silliness of seeing a man talk to an insect. He turned to see the same little curly-haired blonde girl he had seen in the woman's picture. She turned and skipped away, calling out over her shoulder. "I'll go get her. She's my best friend in the whole world."

Ben stared at her in shock, then slowly turned to look at his finger. The butterfly was still there, her wings going lazily up and down. He quickly looked back to see the little girl. There was nothing. No sign of her. He slammed down on his bench, and as he did so, the startled butterfly leaped into the air and flew off.

Lord, the woman was right! Tomorrow he would clean himself up and find an AA meeting. He was definitely losing his mind. Talking to butterflies. Seeing children who were not there. All the booze was getting to him. What would it be next, pink elephants dancing in tutus? Talking faerie dragons named Vern from another dimension? Yes, it was time for serious help.

He sat at the bench, shaking with emotion, trying to clear the crazy thoughts out of his head. A yellow Tiger Swallowtail – was it the same one? – landed on his knee. It was only there a second, then rose in the air to join another butterfly – a Black Swallowtail with vibrant colors splashed against the black of its wings. Together the two of them rose to the air and began to swirl back and forth, a joyous dance, catching currents, tumbling over each other.

Ben watched in stunned disbelief. His eyes saw butterflies, but his mind saw Tessie and her best friend, Eleanor, tumbling in the grass behind their house, laughing and giggling in joy. " No, no. " he whispered to himself. "This can't be. I'm losing my mind."

He raised his hand to the sky, palm up, his fingers extended. In slow, weaving circles, the butterflies descended toward him. They landed on his outstretched, upraised palm.

"There must be something on my hands." he thought. Gently he brought his hand toward his face. The butterflies turned to face him, their wings gently moving up and down as did so.

"Tessie?"

No, no! Come on! This is silly. Ridiculous! Children don't die and become butterflies. Bread doesn't become the Flesh of God. But he could no longer help himself.

"Tessie. If this is really you, come give me a kiss."

The Tiger Swallowtail leaped into the sky and flew away, leaving the Black Swallowtail on Ben's hand. Then the Black Swallowtail took to the sky.

"Yeah, I knew it." Ben muttered under his breath.

The Black Swallowtail turned and headed directly for him. Before he could react, it landed on his cheek. The shock immobilized him. He felt the gentle touch of a butterfly proboscis, touching his cheek over and over again. Then, as quickly as it had happened, the butterfly was in the air with her yellow companion. Dancing on the still blowing gentle breeze, they fluttered higher and higher until Ben could see them no more.

He shook his head at the craziness of this surreal event. This was not real. He lowered his head and looked back to the park. Two small girls in dresses, about fifteen feet from him, were walking away from his bench. One of them was sporting a mass of curly blonde locks. The other had long straight black hair. Hair that was exactly like Tessie's. The little blonde girl turned back to Ben and waved, and as she did so, he noticed the birthmark on the right side of her face.

"Tessie!" he cried out, stumbling to get off the bench. "Tessie!" He lowered his arms to push himself up. As he struggled to lift his tired body from the bench, his head slumped and his gaze dropped to the ground. When he was on his feet, he saw no little girls. The park was strangely empty. He collapsed back on his bench, drew his arms around himself, and began to weep.

He sat and cried for a long time, but he could not tell if was for sorrow or for joy.

1st Place Winner – Writer's Digest 81st
Annual Writing Competition
Inspirational/Spirituality Category

THE SONG OF THE
SAW-WHET OWL

Albert heard the sound as he was watching the sun paint streaks of pink across dark evening clouds. It was a high pitched peeping, in regular intervals. It went up one note in pitch for ten seconds, then stopped.

"What's that?" he asked.

"Northern Saw-whet owl. Pretty, isn't it?" Joanna cupped her hands to the sides of her mouth and perfectly imitated the call. There was silence for a few seconds, then the call repeated, louder and more urgent this time. She smiled. "He thinks I'm another male, challenging him for territory and mating rights."

"How did you learn that?"

"I sat here and listened at night. They only call during mating season. The rest of the year they are quiet and deadly little hunters."

"Little?"

"Oh, yes. He could fit nicely in the palm of your hand." Albert tried to imagine an owl so small it would fit nicely in his hand.

"It's so beautiful here tonight. It's a shame you can't see it."

"I have my memories. I see everything clearly." She laughed. "I just have to close my eyes."

It was a joke. A joke because she was blind and her eyes would not open. Blind and terribly scarred from the acid that her ex-husband had thrown in her face when she discovered he was cheating on her. She confronted him in the garage late one night and a furious argument ensued. In anger he reached without looking for the nearest thing that he could find to throw at her. What his hand found was a bottle of acid he used to etch electronic circuit boards. His aim was perfect.

They sat in silence, enjoying the warmth of a late spring evening. "I don't know how you ever forgave him for what he did to you."

"He asked me to forgive him." Joanna's voice was quiet and factual. "What else could I do?"

"You *could* have told him to go straight to hell!" Albert growled, fidgeting with a cup of coffee on his lap. "That's what I would have told him. Straight to hell with you, pal!"There was another long silence. "How can you forgive someone for doing something like that to you?" His voice was subdued and filled with confusion.

"There is no *how*, Albert. You forgive. It's a choice, not a feeling."

The owl sang again. In the yard below, a cautious deer approached a feeding tub full of cracked corn. Albert leaned over and whispered in Joanna's ear, letting her know the deer was at the feeding tub.

They sat in silence until the doe left. Albert shook his head and sighed, his arms crossed over his chest.

"Weren't you angry with him?"

"Heavens, yes!" she sighed, rising from her seat. Her cane in hand, she tapped her way gently toward her back door. "It took me three weeks to call him back and forgive him after he called me from prison." They entered into the living room and sat down together. She heard him plop down on one of her chairs and turned to the sound. "I didn't say it was easy, did I?"

"Okay, if it's a choice and not a feeling, how do you feel about him right now?"

The question caught her off guard. She really hadn't thought much about Mike since the day ten years ago that she had called him back and told him that she forgave him. He was in prison. She forgave him and life moved on.

She sat without speaking, facing straight ahead, her sightless eyes welded shut by scar tissue. Albert studied her as she sat with her thoughts, remembering the shock of first seeing her. He had come to repair her roof. When she met him at the door he was startled. She looked as if someone had ripped away the skin on her face in a brutal swatch from left to right across her eyes. This was what the acid had done, leaving a nasty looking red scar. As he watched, her fingers tightened on the cane and it began to tap on the floor. Harder and harder, until she gave it one last solid thump.

"I'm still mad at him," she managed to mutter. "God forgive me, I'm still mad at him."

"But you said you have forgiven him. How can you be mad at him?"

"I told you. Forgiveness is not a feeling." She rose from the chair and felt her way over to the kitchen counter. Working her way up the cabinets with her hands, she located her tea, found the tea kettle, and put it on the stove. Her hands deftly felt their way to the stove's knobs. She turned on the burner and waited to hear the *whoosh* of gas lighting. "It's something I have to do – between me and God. I forgive him every day. Every day I ask God to help me hold that forgiveness in my heart." She sighed deeply and lowered her head. "Some weeks it's one day at a time."

She turned and pointed to the wall of her living room. "Is my Crucifix there?" She didn't wait for an answer. "You know when I realized it wasn't going to be easy? After Mike called me. After he called I would think of that Crucifix every time I prayed. One night it occurred to me that it wasn't easy for God to forgive us either. Look at what it cost Him. Not easy. I kept praying for three weeks after he called me. Every time I prayed I swear a voice was telling me, *'I didn't say it was going to be easy, did I?'* "

Albert rose from his chair slowly. "I should get going. It's getting late."

"No story?"

He hesitated, his hand on the doorknob. It was their routine whenever he came over. He would read from one of her books. She was still not comfortable with Braille. He had begun to read to her after she told him one night how much she missed reading her books. They were halfway through The Wind in the Willows.

"Not tonight."

"That's not like you, Albert. Is something wrong?"

"No," he lied. "I just need to get going. Can I give you a little kiss?" He went to her and kissed her on the forehead. She gave him a smile in return.

"I like you, Albert." She reached out to touch his arms, then let her hands slide down their sides till she could take his hands in hers. "You're a nice man. Always remember that. You're my friend and I like you."

He liked her, too. Much more than he wanted to admit or could get the courage to tell her.

❀❀❀❀❀

A week later he was still pondering their conversation and thinking of his brother. Dave, who thought the next dollar was the only thing life was about. Who had somehow managed to get their father's will changed and cheat him out of half a million dollars. It had been five years since Albert found out that Dave had done this to him. Five years and one punch in the mouth before walking angrily out of Dave's house. Yeah, he had sucker punched Dave real good. Laid him right out on that fancy carpet of his. Then, for good measure, Albert cussed him out, sparing nothing, before slamming the door on his way out.

He bent over a cup of coffee, shook his head slowly from side to side, and sighed. Wind whipped rain in crazy circles around the parking lot of the diner where he was eating breakfast. No roofing to be done today. How do you forgive someone who ruined your life? His life wasn't exactly ruined, but he could imagine a whole different life with that money. But Joanna. To never again see the moon shimmering across the tops of pine trees on a summer's eve. To never again see sunrises and sunsets over the ocean. To miss all the brilliant Spring flowers. His fists clenched in anger at the unfairness of it.

He let his mind wander back over time. Scenes flashed like photographic stills. Standing with Dave in the outfield of the old ballpark behind St. Mary's parish. Playing with a beach ball on the beach of St. Augustine. Christmas. Birthdays. Dave had always been his buddy. When did Dave change? What would make him do such a thing to his own brother? He tried to push the thoughts away, but they refused to go.

One of his workers approached. "We no be work today?"

"No, Miguel. Sin el trabajo de hoy." He made a half saluting motion to the young man waiting at the edge of the table for a reply. Miguel turned and started to walk away. Albert called to him. "Miguel! Papel, por favor." Maybe reading the paper would get his mind off his brother. The paper was days old. Miguel read newspapers to learn English. It was a small town paper, full of the usual small town stuff. Not like the Miami Herald where he had grown up. He looked at the dreary day outside. Would be nice to be in Florida now. He hated the weather in the Northwest. Always seemed to be raining.

LOCAL WOMAN KILLED IN FALL

Another tragedy. He scanned the story, only half interested and ready to throw the paper in the corner and go home. Maybe he would go see Joanna later. They could talk. She might help him understand.

His hands suddenly clenched the paper as he read. He uttered a loud, guttural cry, half moan and half scream of denial. It pierced the air, causing people to turn and look his way.

"Joanna! No, no, no!" He slammed the paper on the table and continued to moan, his face buried in his hands. As a nearby diner tentatively arose from his seat to offer help, Albert thrust himself from the table and dashed out the door.

❀❀❀❀❀

He pushed aside the police tape and used a credit card to jimmy the front door. The house was cool and damp. He ran through the rooms, calling her name frantically, as if his insistent calling could somehow make her appear in the living room. He kept screaming out her name until he collapsed onto her living room sofa, unable to cry, unable to speak in the searing reality of her death.

After a while, he opened the back door and walked slowly out onto the deck. A section of the railing was missing. He stared numbly, then shuffled over to examine it. The wood was rotten. He peered over the edge. The offending section still lay on the ground where it had carried her to her death. As he lifted his eyes again, he saw the grave. It was still fresh, the dirt settled down by the morning rain.

She had always said she was going to be buried in her backyard, even going to war with the township until they relented and gave her permission. His eyes examined the grave. A large and plain stone said: Joanna Perkins. November 7, 1959 – April 25, 2012. "But the greatest of these is love" 1 Corinthians 13:13. Her daughters had kept their promise.

He thought of the many times he had come over and found her standing at the railing, facing the woods she could not see, taking in the sounds and smells of the forest behind her home. She must have leaned forward. The wood was no good. She must have leaned forward. The wood was no good. Leaned forward. The wood was no good. Leaned forward. Leaned forward. Leaned forward. He shook his head and groaned, trying to purge the image of her falling.

When he looked up, a flash of movement startled him, followed by a soft thump. A small, gray ball of feathers lay on the deck in front of the door. It was a bird of some sort. As Albert approached, the bird flapped around in fear, trying to get to its feet. Disoriented, it tried to take off and slammed again into the glass of the door.

Albert was on it quickly. Covering it with his hands, he pulled it close to the warmth of his chest, trying to calm it. The bird resisted for a couple of seconds, then went still. He cautiously opened his hands. It was an owl. An owl so small it fit nicely in the palm of his hand. He opened his hands a little more. The owl did not move. He poked it tentatively with his finger, then realized it was dead.

He shook his head. There were words but no sense. The world was crazy. Was he hearing voices in his head?

"I didn't say it was easy, did I?"

He went inside the house and found one of Joanna's shirts still in her closet. He wrapped the owl in the shirt and went down the steps to her grave. A few swipes with a shovel made a nice size hole. He placed the owl in the hole and replaced the dirt. He stood and stared at the grave for a few minutes, then walked back to his truck. He plucked his cell phone out of its holder and began to dial.

"I didn't say it was easy, did I?"

When the voice on the other end said hello he replied, "Davy? It's Albert. I forgive you." There was no answer. After a long time with no reply, he flipped the phone shut. Turning back to the house, he entered the side door to the garage and began to rummage around. He found a Jerry can, half filled with gas. He trudged down the hallway, studying the house as he walked through it. She had never taken his name off the deed to the house, even after what he had done. Why?

"I didn't say it was easy, did I?"

"Shut up!" Albert growled. He didn't want to hear it. Let her forgive him. He would make sure some small bit of justice prevailed in a senseless universe. The can tilted in his hands. The pungent smell of gasoline filled the room.

"I didn't say it was easy, did I?" Albert's hand paused. A single drop of gas poised on the nozzle, then splashed on the floor. Through the silence came a high pitched peeping sound, set at close intervals. It went up one note in pitch for ten seconds, then stopped. His hand tightened on the handle, then he screamed and blindly flung the can. It crashed through the thin glass of the window behind him and bounced across the deck.

Hours later the police found Albert at Joanna's grave. He was sleeping, his body slumped against the headstone. The sergeant shook his head, trying to understand. There was an odd hole dug in the grave. The sleeping man was holding small dead owl in his hands, pressed against his heart.

A PONY
FOR RAY

Sometimes I sit and wonder how it was that Ray came into my life. I was in my last year of specialty residence at Memorial Hospital and hated just about everyday of it. The ER in which I was training was a constant circus of comforting demanding elderly hypochondriacs and stitching knife wounds in unappreciative gang members with bad attitudes. Would it kill someone to once in a while say *"Thank you, doctor"*? Somehow I had lost sight of just why I was practicing medicine and why I wanted to be a doctor.

Ray wasn't very talkative the night I first met him. Earlier that evening I had watched a teenage stabbing victim die in the ER, despite our best efforts to save him from the wounds that laced his body and opened up his vital organs. Death is our enemy, and that night the enemy had won. I was in the diner across from the ER, sitting in a booth near the door. My mind was running over the ever increasing feeling of my life's senselessness when he came in. I heard the door creak and looked up out of curiosity. Ray came slowly through the door, walking with a distinct limp. He turned to head for the corner, but the waitress' loud and irate voice stopped him short.

"Hey, you! Don't you even think of sitting down unless you buy something tonight, you hear?"

He froze, then turned very slowly to face her. I'll never forget the look on his face. It was clear that she had embarrassed him, talking down to him so anyone there could hear her. I saw an short, stocky older guy, maybe old enough to be my father, a worn-looking man who appeared to be down on his luck. It seemed to me that a little coffee and maybe a sandwich would go a long way to making him feel better.

"Buy ya a cuppa Joe?" I asked, inviting him with a motion of my head to come over and sit. I tried to sound friendly, despite being bone tired and depressed. He cocked his head to the side and stared back at me. His eyebrows knitted for a second, then he nodded, shuffled over to where I was sitting, and plopped down across from me. I was in the middle of a slice of cherry pie when his coffee arrived.

"Pie's pretty good tonight. Ya want some?" I tried to make it sound offhand.

He didn't answer right away. He put cream and a lot of sugar in his coffee, took a sip, and made a contented sigh. He put the cup down and wiped his mouth with the back of his hand. Then he took another sip and when he put the cup down again, he quietly said "Thanks." I took that to mean yes, so I ordered the pie.

I began to see Ray off and on after that night. It felt odd to call him a friend the first time one of my fellow doctors asked me who he was, but that was probably the best description. Ray doesn't talk much, but he's a great listener, and at that time in my life, I really needed a friend to listen while I complained about the world and my disgust with it. Somehow, after all was said and done, he managed to say something that made me feel better.

After a few months, I got the feeling that Ray had a certain admiration for me as a doctor. He was always telling me how great it must be to save lives and how he wished he had done better in school. He gave me a great deal of encouragement when I was feeling like pulling the plug and just leaving it all behind. In turn, I shared stories with him about the emergency room cases I had seen. Some of them were pretty graphic, but he listened intently. I could see unfeigned interest in his eyes, and sometimes he would say, "You mean you can actually fix something like that?" I remember how amazed he was when I told him how I cut open a gang member one night to reach into his stomach and hold his abdominal aorta until we could get a clamp on him and save his life.

I don't think I ever told Ray this, but I think he's an amazing guy. He was a high steel worker for twenty years. I finally got that out of him after a year of knowing him. Like I said, great listener, but not real talkative. I think he was embarrassed to admit to this college kid that he didn't get beyond high school. What little he did share about his days in high school seemed to be uncomfortable for him to mention.

I don't know what Ray looked like in high school, but he was a pretty good-looking guy when I met him, even underneath his worn out clothes and the constant five o'clock shadow he wore. He told me one night that he was picked on in high school, but I can't imagine that because he looks like he could pound anyone who annoyed him right into the ground. He's a solid man, but perhaps his years on the high steel did that for him. I know I was pretty shrimpy until my senior year in high school. Then, somehow, I mysteriously grew six inches and put on fifty pounds. So maybe he was a bit of a nerd and an easy target.

He told me he started construction work in high school and when he was twenty-one, told his boss he wanted to walk the high steel. The boss asked him if he was sure and then let him go up with a seasoned iron man. Ray said he loved it.

"You know what's best about being up there?" he asked me one day. "Sitting on a girder on the forty-second story of a building you're building and being able to see all of Manhattan." I'll never forget how his eyes lit up the day he told me that. The look on his face told me that he had fond memories of a work he once enjoyed but could no longer do.

"A building you're building." Ray has a quiet pride about him. I could tell that whatever he did in life, he did it well as a matter of principle. He walked the high steel until a freak gust of wind caught him thirty-five stories above the ground. The gust pushed him off the girder he was walking and dropped him thirty feet to a temporary work platform two stories below. On the way down, he bounced off a girder hanging in mid air and broke his back. His right femur broke into so many pieces upon landing that the doctors debated just cutting the leg off. Somehow they managed to save it, but they might have been better giving Ray a prosthesis. He has a hard time walking and told me one day that he is in pretty much constant pain. I didn't understand when he said "I just offer it for souls."

Souls. What is a soul? I don't believe in that religious mumbo-jumbo. I've cut open dozens of bodies and have never seen a soul. I've watched people die and didn't see anything that looked like a soul leaving their body. They didn't go out screaming about falling into a fiery pit of hell either, like some of these money-grubbing, cockamamie TV evangelists claim before they swindle people out of $100 to supposedly keep their souls from falling into eternal perdition.

"Whadda want in life, kid?" he asked me one day. I was a month from graduating in my speciality. Life loomed ahead.

I had to think. I hadn't been asked that question in a while. "I guess the usual. Money. Nice car and house." Then I turned the question on him. "What do you want?"

His eyes took on a faraway look. "A little farm. A small place out in the country. Anywhere. As long as I could have a pony." He stopped to take a sip of his coffee. "I always wanted a pony when I was a kid," he continued quietly.

"A horse? Why?"

"Not a horse. A pony. Something small like me. I could handle a pony. A horse would be too much." His eyes still had that dreamy look. "I always wanted a pony."

❀❀❀❀❀

The story I got from the police was that Ray stepped into a fight. Actually, it wasn't a fight as much as it was three big kids pounding a smaller kid who wouldn't give up his jacket. Ray waded in and started throwing punks around. He was doing good until one of them pulled a knife from under his jacket and stuck it between his ribs. I was on ER duty the night they brought him in. He was barely conscious. It was a bad wound, especially on an old man.

"Hey, kid." He tried to smile through the pain. " Looks like I bit off a bit more than I could chew." He was coughing up blood. "Can't breathe."

"Your lung is probably collapsed."

We inserted a chest tube and the blood gushed out all over the floor. For a split second I was afraid he was going to bleed out on me and die right there.

After my shift was over I shook off my tiredness and went to the room where they had him sedated. One of the nurses had gone to the trouble of giving him a fresh shave. I sat by his bed and looked out the window. Stinking city! I remember that night just wanting to scream at the world. The punks would get away, Ray might die, and no one would care. How could I believe in a God who would let this happen? One of the nicest guys I had ever met and he winds up like this thanks to some worthless punks who would probably never amount to anything more than someone's girlfriend in prison one day.

"Whatcha thinkin' of?" His words broke my thoughts. I turned to him. Maybe he saw the concern in my eyes. "Bad, isn't it?"

"You're fine, Ray. A bit cut up, but your surgeon says you'll make it." I was lying. He was in trouble.

I didn't like the look he gave me. The biggest part of recovery is attitude. I've seen fairly healthy people die because they didn't believe they would live. I didn't like what Ray was saying. I knew his attitude could be the undoing of him. He needed a reason to fight, and life had taken just about every reason he had away from him.

There's a little farm about three hours outside the city where the owner raises miniature ponies. I know about it because I grew up in a small house near that farm. I used to go over once and a while to help the stable owner just to be near the ponies. They are cute little horses the size of a big dog. I had a feeling that Ray had never seen a miniature pony and that one of them would be just what he needed.

Things got pretty crazy when I walked in the hospital with a pony in my arms. The guard on duty yelled at me to stop and began to raise a fuss about bringing an animal into the hospital. I tried to explain to him that hospital rules allow for such visits, even if they are a bit unsanitary. He wasn't hearing any of it, so I turned and resumed walking towards the elevators, hoping the guy would let the issue die and go nurse his coffee. It wasn't to be.

The elevator doors were opening when he grabbed me by the shoulder. I tried to reason with the guy again, but for some reason, he had a serious attitude problem that night. There was just no talking with him. I heard the bell for the elevator ring and without thinking – and being more than a little annoyed with this jerk – I put my foot in his stomach and launched him across the hall. He was just stumbling to his feet as the elevator doors closed.

The nurses on night shift were a little more sympathetic. But between their ohs and ahs they scolded me good for bringing an animal into an intensive care unit. I gently reminded them of the rule that permits such visits, even if they are supposed to be infrequent.

I went down the hall to Ray's room and locked the door.

"Ray," I called out, gently shaking his shoulder. "Wake up. You have a visitor."

As his eyes fluttered open, I bent over, picked up the little pony and held her near the edge of his bed. Yeah, it was unsanitary, but a hospital is an unsanitary place by nature. More people die from diseases caught in a hospital than from what brought them in. And Ray needed this.

"She's all yours, Ray."

He stared at us, still foggy from anesthesia and sleep. "Don't ya want to pet her?"

He slowly gave me a big smile and gently held his hand out for the pony to smell. She nudged his hand with a soft nicker and he ran his hand up and down her face, stopping at the top of her head each time to tousle her mane.

"She's all yours, Ray. I bought her for you. She'll be waiting for you when you get out of here."

He nodded. "Thanks." I could see little pools of moisture around the corners of his eyes. "You're a good kid, Tommy."

Ray was soon sleeping again. I stayed with him until the police came and hauled me away for "assault and battery" on the security guard. They put me in the squad car and put the pony on my lap. Honestly, the cops looked like they were enjoying the whole thing, and they made a fuss over the pony.

In the jail cell there was a lot of posturing and tough talk directed my way, then a muscular gang member I had stitched up recognized me and warned the guys threatening me that if any of them touched me he would kill them.

The borough has a night court for misdemeanors. This way the jail cells are not filled with minor nuisance cases when they are needed for perpetrators of more serious crimes. The judge did a face palm and snorted when I was led in with my pony.

"Now what?" he intoned, looking down from the bench and trying to stifle a laugh.

"He brought this animal into Memorial Hospital, Your Honor." It was the security guard who accosted me at the elevator. "And then when he refused to leave, he assaulted me."

I wanted to walk over and smack him upside his head, just on principle, but instead I told the judge Ray's story and ended by citing the regulations on animals visiting patients. I even quoted him the particular page and numerical designation of the rule, being that it was one that for some reason had stuck in my mind when I read it years ago.

"I'm a doctor, your honor. I know the rules."

The judge scratched his chin for a minute, looking almost amused at the whole scene, then smacked his gavel on the bench and told us all to go home. I think *"Get the hell out of here and don't ever bother me again with such nonsense."* were his exact words as he glared at the hospital guard.

I quit the hospital two days later. Or perhaps I should say that I was unceremoniously thrown out on my rear end. I guess it didn't help that in the middle of his lecture to me, I told the chief surgeon to - well, I won't exactly say what it said because it's pretty nasty - and walked out the door. Strangely, that moment felt like freedom.

I stopped by the hospital daily, checking on Ray's progress. Because he's an older man, his recovery was slower than I would have liked, but he healed nicely, and one day surprised me at the diner just as I was preparing to cross the street and visit him. He had a big smile when he saw me.

"Thought I might find you here." He eased into the booth where I was sitting. "The docs say I'm good to go." He ordered a coffee, and we talked for a while. I was almost embarrassed by how many times he thanked me for the pony. At the end of our conversation, he rose slowly from the table, put his hand on my arm, and smiled.

"Tommy, your work is done here. Now find what you really want to do and follow your heart. I'll be fine." And without another word, he smiled and limped away.

Whatever had been rolling around in me came to a head after the hospital kicked me out. I think it was the look Ray gave me when I showed him his pony. I wanted to see that look again and again. Yes, saving lives is a great reward, but being appreciated is important as well, and I realized that self-congratulation over a job well done can only take you so far. It's a human condition to want a little appreciation, and I decided to go look for it with my diploma in hand.

I found it one day in the oddest of places – a piece of paper blowing down the street that said "La Misión de San Juan Bosco." I was going to toss it in a trash can, but the picture on the front of a doctor examining a child caught my eye. After I read about the mission, I knew I had to go to New Mexico and see if this was what I wanted to do.

Father Mark Johnson started La Misión de San Juan Bosco to minister to poor people in New Mexico. I'm amazed at all he has done here, including a small but impressive hospital and free clinic where I care for the sick. Father Mark is a no nonsense guy who gets things done, but he's also a kind man and a brilliant philosopher, which makes for some very interesting conversations between us. Seems he has an answer for every objection I give him about the existence of God. I'm still wrestling with St. Aquinas' five proofs of God. Pretty amazing stuff. I went to Mass once, just to see what it was like. I didn't understand much, but when I went, it just somehow felt right to me. I 'm pretty sure I'll be going again. There's something compelling about it I don't understand but that nonetheless is drawing me.

I set up a practice in downtown Las Cruces, where I treat people who have the money or insurance to pay for their recovery. After all, I do have student loans to repay, and even though I get a great deal of satisfaction from working at the mission hospital, the bank I owe just wants cash.

I brought Annabelle with me. After my run in with the security guard, I returned her to the farm where I got her and took Ray up to see her when he was discharged. When Ray found out about my interest in the mission, he suggested that I take her with me and give her to the mission. "I've had my time with her, Tommy. Now take her with you to those kids who don't have anything."

She's a great little horse and everyone here loves her. Ray takes care of her. Oh, yeah, he's here. He showed up one day out of the clear blue. I was looking a pair of inflamed tonsils and suddenly got the feeling someone was looking over my shoulder. Fr. Mark lets him stay in a room at the mission. Ray cleans and does some cooking. But most of the time he's here at the mission hospital, taking Annabelle into the rooms to visit sick children.

And no one says a word about it.

THE MOST BEAUTIFUL PLACE
IN THE WORLD

F aron Weber walked along the side of the dusty road, his whole ambling motion the gait of a man in no particular hurry, his eyes scanning from left to right, taking in the vibrant colors of early autumn trees. From time to time he stopped to gaze at the distant Appalachian Mountains with their swaths of colors singing the song of the fall, which only he could hear. How was there still a road like this in America? Everywhere he traveled seemed to be long ribbons of asphalt disappearing into the horizon, a raceway for maniacs seeking to kill themselves. Hardly a road to be found anywhere that wasn't paved over, yet here was this wonderful old dirt road, reminding him of his childhood and the days he walked his dreams down the dusty lane leading to his home.

Stopping at a split rail fence, he clucked at two horses grazing in the pasture inside the fence. One of them ignored him and continued to pull the long grass from around the fence line, but the other perked his ears inquisitively, then began a slow gait over to where Faron stood. From his pocket Faron withdrew an apple, cut it into halves, and coaxed the horse closer with the offered fruit.

"Hey, boy, come on!"

The horse stopped a few feet away and regarded Faron with a wary eye. Faron held the fruit in the flat of his open palm, a tempting morsel in exchange for friendship. The horse finally took him up on the offer, allowing Faron to stroke his neck and mane as he gobbled up the peace offering. Faron closed his eyes and let his mind focus on the sensation of the horse, the wind, the smells of Fall, and all that was right with the world at that moment.

"Hey, mister! Whacha doing?"

Interrupted, Faron opened his eyes to see a young boy, perhaps eight or nine years old, dressed in bib overalls.

"Just stopping to say hello to this horse." He smiled at the lad. "This your horse? He's a fine lookin' animal."

Faron saw the boy for what he was; clean and clear, unconscious of saying anything wrong or nosy, a curious observer of a phenomenon – a stranger on their seldom traveled road – which he appeared to not understand. A man who had stopped feed their horses. In the middle of a nowhere place in the world where people rarely came by, and then they drove by fiercely in fast, shiny cars, racing down the road, kicking up clouds of dust. Faron stood at the fence alone, with a big knapsack on his back and a smile on his face.

"You thirsty, mister? My daddy, he'll get you a drink of water if you're thirsty."

A polite child. A good child. Faron lifted his eyes beyond the boy, his gaze falling on the mountains in the distance, a clean and sweet song singing in his heart. Next to a weathered barn, his eyes took in a simple and unadorned two story house, clapboard siding without paint, a porch held up by rickety looking posts, an old wooden barrel sitting next to the door. Laundry hung in the late afternoon sun. The door of the house opened. A woman emerged, put her hands to her mouth, and called.

"Samuel!" Her voice held concern about the stranger standing all too close to her son. "Samuel. Come here, please!"

The boy turned and ran a few steps, then stopped to call out over his shoulder. "I'll ask Momma if you can have some water. You look thirsty." He was off again, running across the field to meet his mother, stopping in front of her, answering questions Faron could not hear until she suddenly left him behind and walked resolutely to where Faron was standing, his hand stroking the neck of the horse.

"Hello there." Her voice was guarded. Arms folded across her chest. "You mind if I ask what you just gave my horse?"

"Just an apple, ma'am." His voice was apologetic, suddenly realizing her concern. He reached into his coat pocket, drew out another and showed it to her, turning it over between his fingers. "I keep a couple with me." A low, amused chuckle came his throat. "Besides being good eatin', you never know when you might need one to throw at a bear."

"Whaaa...?" The woman's head cocked to one side, mouth slightly open, wondering if she was dealing with someone who was perhaps not all there. She folded her arms across her chest, watching with relief as her husband appeared in the field on the other side of the road. He walked up quietly and stood behind the man.

"I was up in the mountains west of Colorado Springs. Big ol' black bear came out of the woods. I froze, hoping he wouldn't make a move on me, but sure enough, he lit out across the road right for me. I knew I couldn't outrun him." Faron pitched the apple in the air and caught it. "Anyway, I took the apple I was eating and threw it at him." Faron made an exaggerated pitching motion. "Musta got lucky that day. Hit him square in the nose. He stopped dead in his tracks, kinda looked at me like he didn't know what to make of what I just did, then picked up the apple in his mouth and headed into the woods." Faron stared at the woman, sizing up her wide-eyed response. "True story, ma'am. Every word of it."

The woman's face lost a little of its tension. The edges of her mouth curled up a bit, her eyes danced with the absurdity of what she had just heard. "You are either the biggest liar in the world," she snorted, then was laughing with him at his crazy story, "or the most oddly interesting man to walk up this road in a while." She wiped her hands on the apron she was wearing. "Or maybe a little bit of both. What're you doing out here in the middle of nowhere?"

"Just walking, ma'am. Just enjoying this beautiful day."

She stared at him a long time, her eyes making the judgement she needed by looking at the worn shoes and dusty jeans he wore, figuring his age to be maybe in his sixties. There were times in the past when people appeared and you could trust them on sight.

"You know, we have to be careful nowadays." Her hands played at the apron around her waist. "The world seems filled with crazy folks anymore, like the kids we ran off last year." She snorted in disgust. "What would make them pull up here and start throwing rocks at our horses?"

"I think I can trust you, mister. You look pretty straight up and down to me, kind of like my daddy when he was alive. He was a man you could shake hands with and know he would keep his word." She looked Faron straight in the eyes. There not a hint of threat about him.

"Samuel says you're thirsty."

"Not really, ma'am." Faron shuffled out of the backpack he was hauling and let it slide to the ground. "I am a bit tired. Been walking for a while. You mind if I sit here for a spell? I won't make any trouble and then I'll be on my way. Promise."

"Come on up to the porch and take your rest, mister." A different voice from behind him, male and firm. Faron turned to find himself face to face with a man in his forties, a trim man, lean and muscular with the work of running a farm, a well-trimmed beard like his, a large straw hat protecting against the sun.

"I thank you, kind sir."

"Jesse. The name's Jesse Miles." The man stuck his hand out and shook Faron's very firmly when it was taken – a strong handshake, not wimpy or loose like some he had received, a greeting which said, *"I'm a man. I respect you as a man and I expect your respect also."*

"This is my wife, Sarah. And I think you met my boy, Samuel?"

"Yes, sir. Fine young man."

"And you are...?"

"Weber. Faron Weber."

"Well, Mister Weber, we don't get visitors out here much, so when someone drops by, it's kinda a curiosity."

Eight children in all were soon surrounding Faron, the oldest one a strong looking teen age boy, followed by three girls whom he judged to be each a year apart in age, then two more boys – ten year old twins – and then Samuel, whom Faron had met in the field, and the littlest one, the baby of the family, a girl named Sarah, after her mother.

"You're welcome to stay for supper, Mister Weber." Jesse nodded towards the house. "You look like you've been walkin' a while. I imagine you might be hungry. We have plenty enough and then some."

The house was plain and clean inside, the way a house will look when children have chores and are each one assigned to a particular duty. An old sofa, covered in a faded floral print, faced an ample fireplace in which a small fire spread warm cheer on winter's days. On the floor was a large oriental rug which had also lost its color and given in to the drab brown of dirt tracked on it. Everything in the house seemed touched by the color; the room – indeed the whole house – seemed to be all tones of brown and tan and gray, as if there were no such thing as bright colors or paint to give a room sunny disposition. The room had a neat efficiency to it, dusted and clean, with everything in order, but simply without particular color. Faron settled onto the sofa and looked at an array of magazines lined up on a coffee table in front of him. Jesse heard him mumble something under his breath.

"What's that you say?"

"My favorite magazine." Faron picked up a National Geographic held it up. "Beautiful. This is a nice picture, but you have to see these flowers in person to really get their full beauty."

"Really? You've seen those flowers?"

"Yes, sir, and a whole lot more." He started to add something else, but was interrupted by little Sarah making a flying leap into his lap, giggling and playfully pulling on his beard. Faron rose from his seat, lifted her high overhead and gave her a gentle shake before letting her down to the floor. From the kitchen, Mother Sarah entered with a pot filled with mashed potatoes, followed by a procession of children, each carrying a necessary part of the meal; chicken in two baskets, plates, biscuits, napkins, drinking glasses, and a large pitcher of ice tea which seemed almost too heavy for the one twin carrying it.

"Can I be of assistance, ma'am?"

"Why, thank you, Mr. Weber." Mother Sarah stopped her doings long enough to point to the kitchen. "I think there's still a gravy bowl and ladle that needs to come in." She turned back to directing her children in the placement of supper on the table while Faron entered the kitchen and looked for the gravy. When he came out, Jesse and his family were gather ed around the table. After saying grace, the questions began.

"Faron, what in the world brings you to be walking down our lonely old road in the middle of nowhere?"

"What brings you to be living here?" Faron took a long sip of tea, then pushed his glass in the direction of Samuel for a refill. "If you don't mind my asking. I've got a feeling the answer is the same for both of us."

Jesse pushed at a pile of string beans with his fork, thoughtful, wondering how he could describe the feeling he had when he first saw the farm for sale so many years ago. An old farm, weathered and beaten by the years, but filled with potential. A good place to get away from a world that was slowly sapping him of both his family and his mind. "I needed to be here. My family needed to be here. "

"So did I," Faron nodded approvingly. "I saw this fine old dirt road running off the highway, and I knew I had to walk it and see what was waiting."

"You don't have a home, Mister?"

"Mister Weber!" Jesse corrected his oldest son.

"Mister Weber." Corrected, the boy went on, placing his fork on his plate and looking intently into Faron's eyes, his own eyes filled with wonder and questions. "Where do you live? Where's your home?"

"My home is the world. I live wherever I am at the minute. Right now, I live at the home of Jesse and Sarah Miles and all their wonderful children." The children all started to giggle at the word wonderful, all except the oldest son, Scott, who continued to stare intently at Faron.

"Tomorrow." Faron continued, "I will live wherever I wake up. Who knows where that will be? Last week I was living up in those mountains behind your house, just a little bit north of Charlottesville. Today I am here. And here is indeed a fine place to be."

"You're a gypsy!"

"No. I prefer to think of myself as a traveler. There's a whole big, wonderful world out there and I want to see as much of it as I can before I die." Faron stopped long enough to take a bite of chicken before speaking again. "I've seen a lot of wonderful things..." He paused and looked directly at Jesse, sitting at the head of the table "...and I've met a lot of real good people." He leaned back in his chair and winked at Scott. "And a few world class jerks...but fortunately they have been few and far between."

"Jerks? Like...what?"

"Hmmm...like the guy I caught poaching elephants in the African savannah. Nothing I hate worse than poachers. Elephants are becoming endangered now because of guys like him. Elephants. Tigers. Lots of animals. Poaching for money." Faron's mouth tightened. "I came upon him lying in the grass, rifle in hand." There was hardness in his eyes, his forefinger tapped on the table as he continued answering the question. "I knew exactly what he was up to, lying on the ground with a rifle in a game reserve where he didn't belong."

"What happened?" It was Scott, his voice filled with wonder.

There was a long silence before Faron replied. "He never heard me sneak up on him." More silence. "I left him where I found him. And I took his rifle with me."

"You?" Mother Sarah's eyes widened, her voice incredulous. "Mr. Weber, I mean no disrespect, but you don't look...well, you seem awfully old to be bragging about taking on a poacher."

"Years ago." Faron rose from his chair, picked up his empty plate, and then began to pile other plates on top. "I was in my twenties when it happened. Young. Strong." His voice filled with regret. "I just hope didn't kill him. I never found out what happened to him. I left him there and threw his rifle in the Limpopo River." Faron disappeared into the kitchen with the pile of dirty dishes, leaving Jesse and his wife to stare at each other. His voice came through the door before he did.

"I was young and had a temper. I've spent a long time wishing I had done something different." He began to collect the rest of the plates. "Do you want me to bring in that apple pie on the counter?"

Mother Sarah nodded to Faron. "You're an interesting man, Mr. Faron Weber." She leaned forward, her chin resting on her hands, her eyes inquisitive. "Should we be afraid of you, Mr. Weber? I don't quite know what to make of you. You say you killed a man in Africa, or at least you think you did. You wander up to our farm out of the clear blue. You tell fabulous stories that I don't know if I can believe. Who are you, Mr. Faron Weber?"

"A traveler, ma'am. Just a man out seeing the world." He returned to the kitchen, reappearing in a few seconds with a pie in each hand, the still hot plates held in checkered dish towels. "I thank you for your hospitality and I promise you I will be gone as soon as supper is over." He placed the pies on the table, one at each end, and began cutting slices out of the one closest to him. "We all have to meet God someday. I have enough sins on my soul. Don't want any more than I already have."

Jesse leaned back in his chair and smiled. "You should be Catholic, Mr. Weber. That's the reason we have Confession."

Faron's voice was subdued when he replied. "Momma and Daddy were Catholic. I was raised in the Church. Sorta." Pushing his plate from him, he leaned back in his chair, his eyes raised to the ceiling. "I don't know how it happened, but somehow I lost my faith. I liked church as a kid, but somehow when I got older, it just didn't seem to do anything for me." He pushed the chair from the table and made a stiff little half-bow, first in the direction of Jesse, then to Mother Sarah. "If you will excuse me now, I thank you so much for your hospitality and I will be getting along." To which a general ruckus erupted from the table – protests that he not leave, drawn from a united chorus of children's voices.

"Music is an important part of our lives. I think my children would be mighty disappointed if you wouldn't stay to hear them play."

"Well, I certainly couldn't do that now, could I?' Faron replied with a smile. A short stay turned into two hours of music, followed by bedtime prayers and the Rosary. As he led his children in prayer, Jesse watched Faron, noting with interest the silent movement of Faron's lips during each Hail Mary.

After everything was done and the littlest children tucked in for the night, Jesse caught up with Faron at the gate to the road.

"You always leave without saying goodbye?"

"Ahhh..." A pause. Faron's gaze fell to the ground. "I didn't want to bother you folks." He looked off to the distance, to the mountains where the last rays of sunlight streamed through deep purple and pink clouds. His right hand slowly extended to Jesse. "Thanks for everything. You have nice family, sir. You should be real proud of those children, every one of them."

Jesse took Faron's hand in his and held it."Where are you planning on sleeping tonight?"

Faron reached behind his shoulder with his left hand and patted his knapsack. "I have my tent. "I'll set up somewhere down the road." Jesse stared at him, his mouth working, his tongue between his teeth, making sucking sounds as he thought. "I kept you longer than I should have. Why don't you set up in my barn? There's good soft straw there."

Faron started to reply, but they were interrupted by Scott, running through the front door, a great leap to the ground to join his father and put his arm around him. "The little ones are all in bed." He turned to Faron. "I'm glad you're still here, Mister Weber. I really wanted to talk with you." The boy turned to face his father full on, eye meeting eye. "Can he stay the night? I want to hear more about his traveling and all the places that he's seen. Can he? Please?"

"Well, it's up to him. I've invited him to stay in the barn for the night, but I can't make him."

Scott turned to back to Faron. "I'd really like to talk with you, sir.

"Would you stay and talk with me? Please?"

"Well, okay." Faron made a half turn to face the house and began a slow walk towards it. "I'm not sure what you want to know, but I'll be glad to talk with you for a while. And I'll take you up on that offer of the barn."

Scott called out to the figure of Faron disappearing up the driveway.

"Where're you going, Mr. Weber?"

"You said you wanted to talk, son. I figured we could sit a spell on the porch and have a nice chat."

Faron resumed his slow walk toward the house, his shoes scuffing the ground, kicking up pebbles and little clouds of dust in the driveway. When he realized that he was walking alone, he turned back to see Jesse and Scott standing where he had left them, some fifty feet away, their arms moving in wide gestures, their mouths moving in a muted discussion of some sort. Faron slowly strolled back to where they were standing. As he drew closer, he could hear strong emotion from Scott and the words, "I want to talk to him alone." Jesse stopped talking as Faron approached, but the boy kept talking, causing Faron to have to interrupt him to speak.

"Son, if you have something to say that you don't want your folks to hear, then I'm not going to be able to listen to you. It's not right for you to confide something to me that your folks should know about."

Scott didn't move.

"Well....your choice. You can have a sit with me and your Dad and I'll hear your questions, or I'll just head over to the barn and call it a night." Faron placed a friendly hand on Scott's left arm and gave a gentle tug as his sleeve. Scott looked unhappy, his head slowly shook from side to side, his lips clenched.

"Come on, son. I bet I know what's on your mind. You, too, Jesse. I think deep down inside your boy wants to talk with you but he's a little afraid"

"Afraid?" The three began a slow stroll to the porch. "Afraid of what? I've always had a good relationship with Scott."

"I know." Faron eased himself into an old rocker, hearing the satisfying creak of the wicker as it sagged under his weight. "I could see that at the supper table. You're a good father, Jesse, and your children love you. That's why Scott's afraid. He doesn't want to hurt your feelings."

"How?"

"You tell me if I'm wrong, Scott, but I get the feeling that you're planning on leaving the farm and doing some traveling." Faron watched the boy slowly nod his head. "Yeah, I thought so. I saw it in your eyes tonight when I was talking about my travels. I've seen that look before. When I was talking about Africa, I saw your eyes. Eyes of a dreamer, eyes of a man filled with curiosity, wanting to know, to be there, to experience everything for yourself. You can't fool me, son. You're just like I was when I was your age."

"We've been over this before, Scott." Jesse's voice took an edge. "I don't want you leaving here."

"Why?" Faron pulled a pouch of tobacco from his knapsack and busied himself with rolling a cigarette. He gently tapped a pile of tobacco into the paper, spread it out and tamped it down with his fingers, then licked it shut. "Do you need him here, or is there something you're afraid of?" The flare of a match illuminated Faron's face, then slowly dimmed and died out, leaving the bright red tip of the cigarette between Faron's lips. "He won't stay here forever, you know."

"I don't want him out in the world. It's a bad place." Jesse leaned forward in his chair, his eyes filled with intensity – the love of a father wanting to protect his son. "He's safe here. He's loved here."

"Yes. He is very loved here. But you are crushing his spirit."

"I don't care. He goes out into the world and something bad will happen to him."

"Maybe. Life is like that. The good and the bad."

Jesse rose to his feet, animated, his hands gesturing wildly as if to drive away from his house the forces threatening to consume his son. "Look! There's bad people out there. Folks who will gladly steal his faith and seduce him into evil." His hand swept towards the road and beyond, to places in his father's mind; places filled with a host of immoral ills waiting to pounce on an innocent child turned loose in a world he was not ready for. It was a world Scott had not grown up in that would happily destroy his faith and his morals. "I don't want him to lose his faith like...."

Silence. Pause. Embarrassment.

"Like me?" Faron leaned back in his chair and blew a gratified puff of smoke into the air. "I don't think traveling did that to me. I hate to say it, but I think my faith was long gone before I was." He took another drag from the cigarette, the tip a bright red point against the now darkened porch. The glow illuminated sad eyes, reflecting on a life now gone by and unable to be recovered. "I said my folks were Catholic, but that don't mean they lived the faith very well. You've given your boy a precious gift." Faron pointed to Scott with his free hand. "Look at him. He's a fine young man with a good faith. That's what's making it so hard on him. He knows the commandments. Honor your father and your mother. He wants to obey you and he wants to go."

Scott tilted his rocker forward. "You said you were just like me when you were my age. When did you leave? What made you want to go?"

"I've got a feeling the same thing that has the itch in you. Those National Geographic magazines you have inside." Faron chuckled when Scott nodded enthusiastically. "Yeah, I thought so. My Daddy used to get them. Every month a new magazine, a new adventure. Pictures of places I wanted to see and things I wanted to experience.

I told you my folks were Catholic, but they weren't very good Catholics. Their religion pretty much stayed in church after they headed home. Maybe that's why the religion didn't appeal that much to me. Never saw much to it in my folks' lives."

Faron stopped to take a deep drag from his cigarette. The smoke curled from his mouth as he continued talking, making odd little curls of white against the dark of his face in the unlit porch.

"There wasn't much beautiful around our place. Just nasty ol' smelly pigs and a house that always seemed like it needed to be fixed up. Mom and Dad always seemed to be fightin' with each other." His voice lowered, reverent with memory. "But those magazines. Those National Geographics. Every month they'd come to the house in the mail. Got to where I knew almost the exact day they would show up. There were no dirty pigs in them, no barns to muck out. Mountains with snow capped peaks like Kilimanjaro." He paused, his voice suddenly tender with memory and desire to be where he was not. "I've been there, you know." Faron took a deep breath and with a sigh, let a single word that came out like a prayer. "Beautiful."

"When?" Scott's barely breathed question was almost unheard. "When did you go? When did you leave, and did your folks let you?"

"No. My folks never knew I was leaving. I was seventeen, fed up with school and them, and one day I took all the money I had saved up and just started walking." Faron stubbed the cigarette under his foot and leaned back. "I caught a bus to New Orleans and worked my way across the Atlantic working on an old freighter with a captain who was drunk more than he was sober. God knows how he even got that thing from port to port, but he was a hell of a captain." Faron heard Jesse clear his throat at the word "hell."

Faron offered an apology. "Sorry. Bad habit. Not used to being around good Christian folks."

"Where did you go from there?" Scott's voice filled with unfeigned interest.

"Spent my first year in France. I didn't even know where the freighter was going and I didn't really care. All I knew was that it was headed somewhere I wanted to see. I spent the next year walking through the French countryside, but my heart was really in Africa. I went to England after that, found work, and saved up enough money to catch a plane to Kenya."

"Wait a minute." It was Jesse, his voice curt, putting a halt to the discussion. "You can't just jump a ship and wind up in another country. What about passports and green cards and proof of identity?"

"Oh, yeah." Faron snorted, laughing at the memory. "I got in a *bunch* of trouble when we arrived in France. The captain of that old freighter assumed I had my papers in order. The French customs folks were, ahhh...shall we say a little less than amused at this brash young kid who thought he should be allowed to roam the world as he saw fit. Didn't help that I got real snippy with them for just doing their job." He shook his head, chuckling at the memory. "Took three weeks with the U.S. consul to get my papers and they came that close..." Faron held his hand out with his thumb and forefinger touching "...to sending me back to the states. I don't know how, but somehow I managed to talk them out of it and get them to help me get the papers I needed. In the process, I called home and let my folks know I was okay."

"Why?"

"Why what?"

"Why did you go?" Jesse tapped his pipe against the side of the rocker and ground the ashes under his shoe to be sure they were out. "What were you looking for? What was the point?"

"I told you. I wanted to see Africa. Honestly, I thought I would find the most beautiful place in the world there." Faron's voice lowered to an almost reverent whisper. "That's what I wanted. I wanted to find the most beautiful place in the world and settle down. Marry. Raise kids and every day stand in my doorway at the end of the day and see the most beautiful place in the world. A place where I would live and be buried." Jesse slowly rose from his chair.

"But you didn't find it, did you? Because if you did, you'd still be there, wouldn't you?"

There was a long silence between the men. Jesse turned to his son. "It's getting late, Scott. We've got hay to do tomorrow." With his hand on the door, he turned to Faron. "You're welcome to breakfast tomorrow before you go. Have a good night's sleep."

Jesse was halfway through the front door when he heard Faron softly call his name.

"You're right, you know." He inched closer to Jesse. In the background he saw Scott stop, then walk back towards them. "I've seen some fantastic sights. But I didn't find the most beautiful place in the world. You know why? Because I finally figured out that wherever I went, people and places are all the same."

He turned sharply, picked up his knapsack, and headed into the night, leaving Scott to stare at him in confusion as his silent figure disappeared towards the barn.

"Would you like some help baling that hay?"

Jesse looked up from his coffee, pushed his breakfast dishes toward the center of the table, and rested his elbows where the dishes had been, his head propped on his folded hands. "That's mighty nice of you to offer, Faron." He pursed his lips, thinking, running over in his mind the unexpected offer. "You sure you feel up to it, old timer? It's pretty hard work. Our equipment isn't the most modern in the world." He took another sip from his cup. "And I have to let you know – I can't pay you. Things are pretty tight on most farms nowadays. The big corporate farms have all but driven us small farmers out of business."

"Not looking for pay." Faron collected his plates from the table and headed to the kitchen. He turned at the door. "Would you mind if I stayed here a couple of days and helped out? It's nice here. I'd just like to stay a couple more days – if you don't mind."

Faron disappeared through the kitchen door. Jesse looked at his wife, his eyebrows raised in question, a bit of a smile playing around his lips. Before she could respond, the children seated around the table began to speak up, letting their fondness for their unexpected guest be known.

"All right then, let's get to it. We've got work to do," Jesse announced when Faron reappeared. "If you really want to help, we need the alfalfa cut. I've got a hundred acres across the road that needs to be in by Saturday. I was out checking it yesterday when you showed up. It's ready to harvest – *if* you can drive a tractor. There's an old John Deere in the barn. You ever operate a tractor, or are you gonna kill yourself on it?"

Faron laughed.

"Son, I was driving tractors on our farm before you were a gleam in your Daddy's eye."

"Okay, then. So you know what to do, but I'm gonna tell you what I want, just to be sure. Cut half the field today. You should finish that much by about two o'clock. Then hitch up the silage wagon and blow the windrows into the wagon." Jesse came close to Faron, his voice firm. "I'm serious about this next part. That old tractor's a bit cranky. You have any problems with it – you turn it off! I don't want to come check on you and see you fiddlin' around with it with the PTO still running! You understand?" Jesse lowered his voice. "I saw a man killed like that. You take your time and do things right. We're in no hurry here."

When Jesse came by at noon, Faron had already hitched the silage wagon to the tractor and was slowly working his way down the windrows. Jesse stood and watched him in amazement. The old man was a worker, no doubt about that, and he looked totally comfortable as the ancient tractor bobbed along the rows, tossing Faron gently up and down on the seat. When the tractor drew near, Jesse held up a basket of food and a bottle of ice tea and made a motion with his head for Faron to head over to where he was standing.

"Good grief, old man. You got a pile of work done this morning!" Jesse handed the basket up to Faron. "Maybe I shoulda asked you to do the whole field."

"I still could."

Jesse shook his head. "Naaa...get that silage in the silo. You can do the other half tomorrow." With admiration he surveyed the work the old man had accomplished that morning, letting a low, appreciative whistle escape through his teeth. "Where'd you learn to work like that?"

Faron peeked in the basket before answering."My Dad. He never tolerated any goofing off around the farm." Faron placed the basket on his lap and pulled out a large sandwich, stuffed with ham and cheese. "We either got the work done he told us to do, or we suffered the consequences." He stopped for a large bite from the sandwich, chewed thoughtfully, then continued. "He showed us all the tricks to getting the most out of a day. We knew what he expected and we did it." He waved his hand at the field behind him. "Pfffft....that was easy."

It was on that day, when he saw how the old man worked and how happy he seemed by the end of the day, Jesse opened his heart and his home to Faron. For the next couple of months it seemed that all Faron did around the farm came easy, including his time with Jesse's children. He talked freely and easily with them, sharing their stories and questions with interest.

What came as no surprise to Jesse was Faron's response to their geography lessons. Faron eagerly shared his extensive knowledge about places he had been and people he had come to know. He didn't just know about the places, he was a wealth of interesting trivia and facts, which he enthusiastically shared with Jesse's children.

Through the fall and into Thanksgiving and the joy of Christmas, Faron became more and more like the grandfather that Jesse's children had never known. He became a comfortable part of the family, helping with the household chores and sitting attentively as the children practiced their instruments in the evening. At prayer time he was quiet and respectful. One night he let little Sarah show him how to pray the Rosary, although he still remembered it from heart. When they were done, she put the pink beads in his hand, telling him they were his to keep.

It was on an early spring morning, a few days after the family had celebrated Faron turning sixty eight, that Jesse took Faron aside in the barn before they broke for lunch.

"I need to talk with you, Mr. Weber." His use of the formal name gave hint to Faron that Jesse was upset about something. He nodded his head and leaned back against the wall of the barn.

"You know I don't want Scott leaving here."

"Yes, sir."

"Well, sir, I'd appreciate it if you would stop with all the tales of your wandering around Africa." Jesse took a couple of slow steps towards Faron as he cleaned his hands on an old rag. "He gets that look in his eyes – a look I don't like seeing – every time he hears you talk about Africa. No place else. You talk about Europe and South America, and he's fine. But there's something about Africa that seems to get under his skin. I'm having a hard enough time trying to keep him here without your tales getting him all fired up."

"It's a beautiful continent, Jesse. Wild and free. Lots of good people there. And some danger as well. But a lovely place to see and live in."

"I imagine it is." Jesse tossed the rag onto his work bench and sat on a nearby bale of hay. "You know, I got those National Geographics to help Sarah home school the kids." A long, tired sigh came from his lips. "I never expected them to cause me the trouble they have. Not so much with the others, but Scott...." His voice drifted off.

"He's a dreamer, Jesse, just like I was. But there's a difference. I never had parents like you and Sarah. There wasn't anything to keep me around." Faron started a slow walk toward the barn doors. "He'll get to Africa, Jesse. He'll get to see what he needs to see and then he'll come home and he'll stay."

Jesse was on his feet, his voice raised. "Faron, do you know what Scott told me the first night you were here? He said that when you leave, he wants to go with you." Jesse took two angry strides towards Faron. "And last night he told me he is planning to leave when you leave. He said he wants you to take him with you to see the world." He threw his hands in the air and wheeled away from Faron. "I don't want to argue with my son." His voice lowered. "But I don't want him leaving either." He came back to stand in front of Faron, working his lips with his teeth, working through his emotions. Finally a long sigh seemed to let it out all the anger with it.

"Look, Faron. Sarah and I have really enjoyed having you with us. And I won't lie to you, you've been a tremendous help around here. And my children love you." Another long sigh. He walked slowly over to Faron and put his hand on his shoulder. "I just don't know what to do with Scott. He says he's going with you when you leave here, no matter what I say."

"No." Faron's denial was absolute and firm. "He's not. He's not – because the next place I'm going to from here, he can't come with me."

It was early in April when Jesse found Faron sitting still and quiet on the porch. They had been out mending fences– Jesse holding the heavy split rails while Faron drove nails – when Faron put the hammer down and walked away, telling Jesse over his shoulder he wasn't feeling well.

"I'll be back in an hour or so, just let me rest a bit."

But he didn't return, not in an hour, not in two hours, until Jesse drove in the last nail and headed at a half trot to the house. Faron was in the old green rocker, his old coat drawn up around him as if to ward off the death that had taken him, his eyes open and staring out towards the mountains he loved. In his left hand was Sarah's pink Rosary, a bead held between his thumb and forefinger. A gentle shake told Jesse the old man was gone.

In Faron's bedroom, Jesse found a letter lying on the dresser. He walked slowly down the steps and into the kitchen where Mother Sarah was peeling potatoes. He took her hands in his, stopping her in mid-peel. He turned her gently to him, smiling with a sadness which made her ask if something was wrong. He pulled her close in his strong arms, burying his face in her hair so he could whisper in her ear. He struggled to maintain his composure as he shared the sad news with her.

"Faron passed away." He felt her body tense, a small gasp came from her lips, followed by a single whispered word.

"No!"

"He's sitting on the porch in the old rocker. I need you to keep the kids in the house until we can talk to them. They're going to be mighty upset."

Jesse –

If you are reading this, then I am gone and you found this note as I have planned you should. I thank you for your hospitality and for sharing your lovely family with me. I think the last time I saw such closeness among family was with the Mandinka tribes in West Africa. You have something special here, and I don't blame you for wanting to keep it as long as you can, but your children cannot remain young forever.

Don't be afraid to trust Scott. He's more level-headed than I was when I was young, and he has a stronger faith than I ever had. That faith will go with him wherever he goes in the world. I would be surprised if he ever got himself into any real trouble.

When I was young, I left my folks and set out to find the most beautiful place in the world. I knew it was out there. I just had to find it. When I found it, I would settle down, get married, and raise a family. But somehow I never found it. I've been to a lot of beautiful places and seen a lot of incredible sights. But I never found that place until I came back home a couple of months ago.

Home, you see, is not too far from here. My folks had a farm over in the next county, and that's where I was heading back from when I met you and your family. I found out last year that I have Hodgkin's lymphoma and don't have a lot of time left. When I found out, I started back home from Nairobi. I had to come home and see the old place one more time, but it was gone. Someone bought the land, knocked down our house, and put up a strip mall.

You might be wondering why I wanted to stay and help out around here. It's really very simple. I found the most beautiful place in the world, right here in my own neighborhood after all these years of looking all over the world for it. I just wanted to stick around for a little while and enjoy it.

If you look in my knapsack, you will find a manila envelope. Remember when I said that Scott would see Africa? A man can save a lot of money when he doesn't have much he needs. I'd be real pleased if you took Scott to Africa for a week. But you decide. I won't tell you what to do with your family, but I think the trip would cure his fever a bit. It's your money – do as you please with it.

Thank you for letting me be part of your family.

Faron.

PS. There's a special note for Scott. Please see that he gets it. It's important he get it.

Jesse folded the letter and slipped it into his pocket. Carefully he pulled back the flap of Faron's knapsack and gently rummaged around until he found a large manila envelope, buried in the bottom under personal items. He undid the clasp and peered inside, then slowly descended to the dining room. At the dinner table he turned the envelope upside down. Gently at first, then with increasing force he shook, shaking loose the bills clinging inside.

Currency from several countries covered the table. A great collection of money, saved up from work done all over the world. Each currency neatly folded and wrapped with a large rubber band. Jesse was counting a large stack of American hundred dollar bills in stunned silence when Scott came through the kitchen door and quietly walked over to the table, astonishment on his face.

"Dad?"

When Jesse looked up, tears were welling in his eyes.

"Mister Weber's gone, son."

"Gone? Where did he go?" Confusion – then seeing his father's tears, the sudden realization. "No! No!" An anguished cry, muffled as Jesse quickly drew his son to him and let him cry. Mother Sarah appeared from the kitchen, followed by the twins. From the top of the stairs the other children appeared one by one, drawn by the commotion downstairs.

By the time Jesse had his children comforted and the crying had settled, Scott was nowhere to be found in the house. Jesse went upstairs first, but Scott was not in his room. Jesse thought he might be in the back field by the tree where he liked to go and think over his problems, but he was not to be found there either. It was on the front porch that Jesse found him, sitting next to Faron's body in a rocker he had pulled up next to the old man, his hand resting on Faron's hand. Jesse eased the front door shut and stood by his son, his hand on Scott's shoulder.

Minutes went silently by before Scott spoke.

"Did you know that on a clear night on the African savannah, with no lights from the city, the whole sky is filled with stars. It's not like here, where you see patches of black. There's not a place in the whole sky that doesn't have dozens of stars. Big stars, little stars..." Scott's voice broke, but he continued on. "Mr. Weber told me you can hear the lions roar every night "

Scott turned and looked into his father's face.

"Did he tell you his stories while you were working in the fields? Did he make it seem like if you opened the front door you wouldn't see this dusty old farmhouse? There were some days, I swear I half expected to open the door and see zebras in our front yard."

In silence Jesse passed over Scott's note and motioned for him to come inside. Once inside, Scott stared at the unfolded paper for a long time, as if the words on it were written in a language he could not understand. Suddenly and without a word, he wheeled and bolted up the stairs to his room, two steps at a time, slamming the door shut behind him, leaving the paper to fall to the floor in his wake.

Still holding her children, Mother Sarah made a motion to Jesse with her right hand, beckoning him to pick it up and bring it to her. Smoothing the paper between her fingers, her face broke into a soft smile as she read Faron's last message to Scott.

"The most beautiful place in the world is
any place where there is love."

DIRTY OLD DOG

Jill was on a rant again. Bill Franknell leaned back in his overstuffed easy chair, closed his eyes, and let his daughter drone on. He had learned a long time ago that no response would satisfy her. Everything about his life bothered her. The yard was not nice. The trees needed trimmed. Today it was the house again and for some reason, she was really on a roll.

"This is the house you grew up in." His voice weary from listening to her complaints.

"No, it's not!" Her disgust was loud and pointed. "It's dirty and filthy and there's dog hair everywhere." Jill turned to stare at her father. She flung her right hand in a circle around her, pointing out the source of her anger. "Mom would shit if she saw this mess!" In her anger and exasperation, her voice particularly emphasized the word "shit."

Bill stared at his daughter. When did she start using language like that – especially to him? An angry response rose from within, then died in his throat. What good would it do to escalate her anger with an angry response of his own?

He allowed a long thirty seconds to go by in silence before responding evenly.

"Charlie's a German Shepherd. They shed a lot."

"You need to get rid of him," she mumbled flatly, glaring at the dog lying on the floor beside Bill. "Dad, he can hardly walk anymore! What good is he? If a burglar broke in here, he'd probably pee himself." At the mention of his name, the old German Shepherd had raised his head slightly and opened one eye to regard Jill. His drew his upper lip back and made a slight growl, then closed his mouth and slowly shut his eyes. Always good to let the enemy know that you are on to them.

"Did you see that?" Jill exclaimed. "He growled at me! He threatened me!" She took an angry step towards Charlie, who responded with another growl.

"Smart dog," Bill responded in a low voice. "He knows who likes him and who don't." Bill leaned over to scratch the old dog's head. "I didn't keep him to scare off burglars. I kept him because he loves me." The dog stretched out and yawned, extending his front paws far in front of his body. At age fourteen, and despite the aging thinness of his body, he was still a handsome dog.

Bill did his best to care for Charlie. At seventy pounds, he was a large dog, but he moved slowly on painful arthritic joints that slowed him down. He turned to look at Jill and give her another small growl before laying his head on his paws. He gave a deep dog sigh and closed his eyes.

"Stupid mutt," Jill mumbled under her breath as she turned to the refrigerator and began to rummage through it. "Good Lord, Dad, there's moldy food in here."

Jill reached under the sink to pull out a trash can. She picked up the offending sandwich between her thumb and forefinger and dropped it in the garbage, complaining under her breath loudly enough that Bill could hear her.

"If you don't like the way I keep the house, don't come over." Bill responded quietly, but his eyes were filling with weary anger.

"We all promised Mom we'd keep an eye on you after she was gone."
She turned back to the dirty refrigerator with a wet dish towel and began to rub
down the shelves. "You ought to be in a home." she mumbled under her breath,
not realizing how loudly she spoke in her anger.

"I heard that." It was an accusation.

Jill froze, momentarily embarrassed, then slowly rose from her knees to
face her father. "It's true, Dad. You can't take care of yourself anymore. Every
time I come over here, the place is a mess. If nothing else, it's unsanitary. You're
gonna catch something living like this." She turned her attention back to the
mold festering on the refrigerator door.

"I'm eighty-four years old. How much longer do you think I have to
live?" Bill reached for his cane and used it to help himself push up and out of his
chair. "I've only got a few years left. When Charlie goes, I'm going with him."
Walking slowly over to the door of the kitchen, he stopped a few feet from his
daughter and stared directly into her eyes.

"Why do you always come over here and complain?" His voice was soft
with concern. "Jill. What is it? What's bothering you?" He asked the question,
but he knew the answer. Like so many times before, Jill stared at him quietly
without a response to his question, then turned quietly back to the fridge and
continued wiping. Why couldn't he get her to talk to him?

"Your brothers don't act like this when they come over." He watched her
hands move angrily over a dirty shelf in the refrigerator.

"No, they don't." She gave the shelf a particularly hard swipe. "Maybe
they're afraid you'll cut them out of your will. May they just don't want to cause
waves." She finished wiping the shelf and bolted upright to face her father again.
"You know who they *do* complain to?" Her finger was pointed right at her
father's nose. "Me! I'm the one they come to with their complaints about how
nasty this house is every time they come over. I get to hear it all. You don't hear

their complaints because they dump them all on me! Just like they did when we were caring for Mom."

She tossed the paper towel into a trash can, retrieved her coat and umbrella from the chair across from where her father had returned to sit, and headed for the front door. Stopping at the door with her hand on the doorknob, Jill turned to look at her father. "I'm going to get you into a home, Dad." Then she headed out into the December snow, calling out over her shoulder. "It's for your own good. You need someone to take care of you."

"I have a home. Right here." But she was already gone. Bill banged his cane angrily on the floor. "Next time she comes here, I want you to bite her in the rear end! You hear me, Charlie?"

At the sound of his name, the old dog wagged his tail slowly, thumping it on the floor as turned to look at his master. A grunt escaped his lips, as if to say he perfectly understood the order given to him. Bill reached for a Rosary lying on the table next to his chair. He fingered the beads lovingly, letting them roll over his fingers as he thought of Jill.

"Whatever happened to honor your father and mother?" he mumbled to himself. But he knew exactly what had happened. After Lorene passed away, Jill had gone slowly downhill. A sigh escaped his lips as he thought of the fact that she hadn't been to Mass for years. The last Mass she went to was two years after Lorene's funeral. She refused to even take him to church, pushing that duty off on her brothers. Billy and John brought him unbelievable tales of finding her drunk on the weekends.

He slowly began the Apostle's Creed. He prayed for a while, but his mind wandered off and finally settled onto more pleasant memories of days long past. Charlie as a puppy. A big ball of love with ears far too big for his body. Everyone had a good laugh when they first saw those ears. Ah, but if they could only see that heart. There was never a better friend in the world than Charlie. So many memories. How long had Lorene been gone before those nice young kids from Mary Queen of Heaven parish came by? It wasn't long. Maybe a week. They were the CCD kids he had taught for years. When they heard about Lorene's death, they came by to pay their respects and to pray a Rosary with Bill for her repose.

They kept coming back for a while, but the visits slowly died away. All except for one girl. Bill could see her face in his memory, but somehow her name escaped him. He smiled to himself as he remembered the day she stood in his doorway, holding an enormous bundle of tan and black fur.

"I thought you might like to have a little company." She put Charlie on the floor. The puppy shook himself, licked Bill's outstretched hand, then promptly left a puddle on the floor. Somehow that amused Bill to no end.

"Nice dog ya brought me," he laughed.

"I'm sorry, Mr. Franknell." She turned to head for the kitchen, but Bill was already there, tearing off a paper towel from the roll. "Let me do that, Mr. Franknell." She gently but firmly took the roll of towels out of his hands. "Why don't you go play with the puppy? See if you like him. He really is a nice dog, even if he did mess on your floor."

He was more than a nice dog. It didn't take long for Bill and Charlie to become inseparable. People used to say to Bill, "Boy, that dog really loves you." and he would reply, "Not as much as I love him." Somehow the ache in his heart managed to subside over the years. Charlie did what he was supposed to do – fix Bill's broken heart.

It was three days after Christmas when two young men dressed in official looking uniforms with white shirts and black ties showed up at Bill's door. Bill looked them over suspiciously, then noticed an old friend from his parish standing behind them.

Chief Wally Johnston had joined the parish thirty years ago as a convert. At coffee hour one morning, the two men were introduced and became fast friends, mostly due to their shared military experience. Bill had marched through Europe with Patton. Chief Wally, as everyone called him, was a large, easy going man who had slogged through the jungles of Vietnam. Thirty years younger than Bill, he was awed by the older man's WWII stories. Together the two of them could kill hours sharing military reminiscences. People often said if you wanted to find either one of them, go to the church first. It was there that they both kept their promises to serve the Lord faithfully if He would just get them home safe and in one piece.

Bill couldn't think of a time he hadn't seen Wally with a smile. But today Wally wore an expression that spoke volumes, all of them bad.

"Wally, what's going on here?" But Bill already knew the answer. The last time he had seen such sadness in Wally's eyes was at Lorene's funeral.

"Bill, you have to come with these men."

Bill took an involuntary step back and shook his head. His lips tightened and he glared at Wally.

"You can't make me." His fists involuntary clenched at his sides.

Wally's hand slowly rose like some ancient sea monster called from the deep. He held a court order face forward so that Bill could see the print on it. "I can't do a thing to stop this, Bill. Jill covered all the bases. She's putting you in Northfield Meadows. Says it's for your own good." The young men looked away uncomfortably.

Bill stood in the doorway, clenching his teeth as he digested the bad news. "Wally, you better be glad I'm not twenty years younger or you and I would be out there rolling around in the yard, court order or not."

"I know, Bill." Wally lowered his eyes and shook his head. "You don't think I'm here because I want to be, do you? Jill made that new family court judge order me to come along in case you made trouble." He paused and gave a deep sigh. "Bill, what in the world happened to that daughter of yours? She was the nicest little kid I ever knew and now she's a witch on wheels."

There was a long silence. Bill was godfather to Wally's three sons, and Wally had always been close to his family. He remembered Jill holding onto Wally after Lorene's funeral and crying her eyes out. The two families were very close. And now this.

The two young men with Wally remained motionless. They had moved to the side of the door out of respect for the conversation going on between the two old friends. One stared at the ground and made shuffling motions with the toe of his right foot. The other had turned away and was looking at the bare winter forest outside Bill's house.

"I don't know, Wally. Ever since Lorene died, Jill hasn't been the same." Bill turned back to the house, moving slowly on aching legs. "We all got past it somehow. I don't know. She won't talk about what's buggin' her, she just comes over here all the time and gripes about how nasty the house is, even when it's clean. Whenever I bring up Lorene, she changes the subject." He trudged toward an open door in the corner of the small house. "I'm gonna pack a few things. You okay with that?" He shuffled to his bedroom and emerged ten minutes later, pulling a small traveling bag on wheels.

"Come on, Charlie. We've got a new home now."

"Bill."

Long pause. Wally's voice was filled with regret. "Bill, you can't take Charlie with you. It's a nursing home. He's gotta stay here."

"What? Wally, you can't be serious! Someone has to take care of Charlie. He can't stay here by himself."

"Jill and the boys promised they would take care of him for you."

"Wally!" Bill's voice was pleading. "You can't let this happen. I know what she's planning for Charlie. She hates him. She wants him dead!" Bill's voice was scared and desperate. "Wally, please! You gotta stop her! She'll have him put down!"

Wally put his hand on his old friend's shoulder. "It's okay, Bill" He retrieved some dog food from the kitchen cabinet where it was kept. He returned to the front door and put his hand on back on his friend's shoulder. "Listen. I promise you I'll come back in the morning and be sure he's okay. I just need time to talk to Kate and see if we can keep him for you." Wally's eyes bore in earnestly on Bill's. "I promise I'll be back first thing tomorrow morning."

Charlie spent the night whining for Bill. His best friend in the whole world had left him and he couldn't understand why he hadn't come back. In the morning, he managed to eat a little food and drink a bit of water. Then he went into Bill's room and stretched out beside the bed, whining softly. He was still there when he heard the creak of the door opening. His tail wagging with joy, he moved out of the bedroom as quickly as his sore old legs would let him, expecting to find his beloved master.

What he found was the enemy.

"Come here, Charlie." Jill's voice had an unusual sweetness to it. Charlie saw something in her right hand. The hair along his back rose and he took a cautious step back.

"Charlie!" The voice was no longer sweet. "Charlie, come here. Bill wants to see you."

A rush of adrenalin, produced by anger or fear, can make man or animal forget about bodily aches and pains. Charlie let loose a loud growl and launched himself toward Jill. As she threw up her hands in fear, she unconsciously turned away from the oncoming attack. Charlie took full advantage of her position, sinking his teeth with all his might into her exposed backside. He growled and shook his head before releasing his grip to the satisfying sound of her scream. The arthritis that had plagued him for years couldn't keep him from crashing through the thin screen of the front storm door and disappearing into the woods surrounding the house.

Jill screamed again, then stood painfully to her feet and unleashed a torrent of swear words in the direction Charlie had gone. "You go ahead and run off, you sorry bastard! You won't get far! I'll see to that!" Fumbling through her purse, she found her cell phone and dialed 911. When the police operator answered, she reported being attacked by a vicious dog, possibly rabid, and that the dog was now on the loose in the woods near Monroe Street.

Two hours of searching turned up nothing. Jill impatiently demanded the officers go farther into the woods, but they declined, stating that the dog was probably long gone and they would simply put out an APB for it.

"You can't let him out there." Her voice was insolent. "He's dangerous, I tell you. Do your duty!"

"Probably no more dangerous than you are." Jill turned to see Chief Johnston walking slowly towards her. "You need go home and stop bothering these officers. They have better things to do with their time." Jill opened her mouth to protest. Wally cut her off.

"Go home – now! Before I find a good reason to arrest you for interfering with police business." The look in his eyes told Jill that he would relish any opportunity he could get to carry out his threat.

"You haven't heard the end of this!" she flung at him. She threw herself into her car, slammed it into gear and screeched out of the driveway, throwing gravel everywhere.

Chief Johnston watched the car scream up the road, accelerating far above the 25 MPH posted speed limit, then turned to the nearest officer. "That sure looked like reckless driving to me, didn't it to you?" When the young officer nodded, Wally waited a moment then motioned with his hand. "Well, don't just stand there, son. Go do your duty." The young officer sprinted towards his cruiser.

"And if she isn't wearing her seat belt, you ticket her for that, too!" Wally smiled in satisfaction as the cruiser sped off with lights flashing, secretly hoping Jill would take this to court. Judge Hopkins owed him a favor – one he fully intended to collect.

Chief Wally spent a long time looking for Charlie. He finally called it a night around two in the morning, but after four hours of fitful sleep, he was back in the woods near Monroe Street, tramping through the weeds where he had quit his search, calling Charlie's name as his flashlight speared the darkness.

It was close to nine o'clock when he came upon Charlie, lying next to a downed tree, too weak to get up. Chief Wally knelt beside him and stroked his head gently.

"Poor old Charlie. You're not looking too good." Chief Wally shook his head at what he saw. Charlie looked like he could die at any second. "I bet you'd like to go see Bill, wouldn't you? How about we go see Bill?" At the sound of his master's name, Charlie's tail thumped against the ground weakly.

Wally slid his arms under the dog and easily lifted him up. He was limp and his breathing was ragged. "Boy, Charlie, you're really sick, aren't you?" He strode to the cruiser, put Charlie in the back seat, and headed out for Northfield Meadows with his lights flashing.

Bill was sleeping when Wally entered his room, carrying Charlie against his chest. He looked pale and drawn, very much like corpses Wally had seen at Soudermyer's Funeral Home. Father Luke from Mary Queen of Heaven was standing by the bed. An empty pix lay on the bedside table. Wally looked at the priest and made a question mark with his eyebrows. Father gave Wally a slight smile and a nod, letting the Bill's friend know that Bill was still with them.

"Hey, Bill. You got company." His voice was soft. "Bill, wake up, old buddy. Charlie's here."

Bill slowly opened one eye. Slow recognition crossed his face, breaking into a great smile. Sliding himself slowly away from Wally, he made an empty space on the bed and patted it with his hand. Wally gently lay Charlie on the bed next to Bill. The old dog snuggled up to his master, reached up and licked Bill's face, and then gave a single long sigh. His body relaxed. Bill gave a soft cry and buried his face in the soft fur of Charlie's shoulder, holding the body tightly.

"You're a good friend, Wally." There were tears in his eyes. He took a deep breath and lay back on his pillow. "I'm tired, Wally. I was just waitin' to see Charlie one more time." His voice trailed off to a soft whisper. "Thanks."

Bill's body relaxed and his eyes rolled up. The monitor next to the bed sounded off. Wally reached over, fumbled with it a second, then pulled the plug out of the wall socket in anger. When the a doctor and nurse came in with a crash cart, Wally gently slid between them and the bed. Tears were coursing down both cheeks.

"He's gone, ma'am. Let him be."

Father Luke was halfway through his sermon, talking about his admiration for Bill and his service to the church, when he noticed a movement in the back. It was Jill, pushing through the double doors and standing behind the pews, swaying from side to side. He tried to continue his sermon as if nothing was happening, but he couldn't focus on Jill and his sermon at the same time. After a futile minute of trying to continue, he stopped to regain his composure. That was when Jill spoke up.

"Keep going, Father!" She yelled, striding unsteadily up the aisle. The small crowd in the pews whipped around as one to see where this voice was coming from. "Go ahead and tell them what a wonderful guy my Dad was." As she drew closer, Father Luke noticed something in her right hand. It was a small box. Jill held it up by its handle and shook it at him "While you're at it, why don't you talk about how he loved this stupid dog of his more than his kids?"

Billy and John stood up in the front pew. John moved quickly into the middle of the aisle, blocking her path to the coffin. When she stopped two feet from him he could smell the liquor on her breath.

"Get outta my way. I've gotta give Daddy his dog." She thrust out her right hand, clutching the box. "I've got Charlie, Dad. You want Charlie, don't you, Dad?" Her sudden movement made her lose her balance. Reaching out to catch herself, she stopped her fall as the box caught the edge of the pew. When it did, unseen to everyone, the lock sprung on it.

"Sis!" John hissed at her. "Not now. Not at Dad's funeral" He approached her with his arms open, his voice quiet. "Come on, we can talk about it later."

"Later my ass!" Her voice lifted in alcohol-fueled rage. "We'll talk about it now!" A torrent of angry words spilled from within. The raw pain of her mother's death. Screaming accusations against the God who let her mother slowly and painfully die over four years from a cancer that would neither respond to treatment nor have the decency to kill her quickly. A father who was always at Mass and never wanted to talk with her about it. The words flowed freely, as if from a script, but there script existed except the pain of a heart unable for years to unburden itself. A heart that turned within itself when neither parish members nor close friends like Wally never came to visit. When people turned away from her probing and angry questions about God's goodness. When a priest overwhelmed with duties somehow never made it to her house, despite his good intentions. Mesmerized, the crowd listened with increasing pain as the accusations flew towards John, Fr. Luke, and the body lying in the coffin, all generously punctuated by profanity. She turned to face the audience and held up the box.

"Yeah, Dad was a great guy, if you were part of his church. All he wanted to do was to go to church and be with this stupid dog of his." Whipping around, she made an unsteady move toward the coffin. "Here, Dad. Take your dirty old dog!"

John made a move to intercept her. As he reached out to grab her, she stepped quickly to one side, pushing him with her left hand, and flung the box at the coffin as she fell to the floor.

The box hit the top front edge of the open coffin, and with the latch no longer holding it together, broke apart. Borne by the momentum, a bag of granulated white powder flew out of the container, hit the back of the coffin lid, and burst open. It covered the body like a newly fallen snow as the broken pieces rattled against the lid of the coffin and rebounded onto the floor. Jill lay on the floor, a broken puddle of drunken rage and sorrow. When John knelt down and tried to embrace her, she flailed away at him, screaming and swearing. Finally she stopped and allowed him to hold her as she wept freely. After several minutes, he managed to gently get her to her feet and take her outside. Billy followed behind, his face full of confusion and embarrassment.

Silence.

That terrible moment when there are no words possible. That time when in the dynamics of the moment a deep, dark secret has made itself known. Something that no one expected to hear and to which there is no response. Deafening, accusatory silence swept over the room. People looked down, looked away, looked anywhere but at each other.

Finally, as if cued by some off stage prompt, Father Luke and Chief

Wally both moved simultaneously to the coffin. Father stopped and stared. He shook his head silently, then placed his sermon papers on the body and gently lowered the coffin lid. With an audible sigh he walked slowly back to the altar. Chief Wally stared at the closed coffin.

"I'm sorry, Bill," he intoned softly. "I had no idea she was being eaten up like that." He placed a hand on the closed lid and made a soft rubbing motion on the top of it. "I promise you, I'll do everything I can to help her." He turned from the coffin and began to walking to the back where Jill and John were.

In the background he heard Father Luke begin the safe, familiar prayers of the Eucharist and the rustling movement of people settling back into their pews.

5th Place Winner – Writer's Digest
82nd Annual Writing Competition
Inspirational/Spirituality Category

BOBBY,

TORRINGTON BULLDOG

He was out of place, surrounded by the long, lean faces of pit bulls trapped in cages next to his. His face was lined with vivid red scars where other fighting dogs had taken their toll on him. We managed to get them into the transport cages without getting bitten or hurting the dogs. It was messy and unappealing work. Everyone I've ever met in animal control was there because they love animals, and this kind of thing gets us a bit barmey around the edges. The drive back was quiet. No one likes to talk about it.

"What kind of nutter does this sort of thing?" It was Andy. He had drawn the short straw for euthanizing that day and he was not happy about it. No one likes the job, but Andy in particular despises it. He once gave me a tenner to take his place, but he wasn't getting out of it today. "Bloody bastards!" he mumbled loudly under his breath.

All the dogs were to be put down. Andy quietly loaded a dart into the tranquilizer gun and walked up to the first cage. The dog lunged at him, bouncing off the mesh of the door and snarling defiantly. There was a soft whoosh as compressed gas sent the dart to its target. Five minutes later Andy loaded the limp body onto a cart and headed off to the gas chamber, still cursing under his breath.

I leaned back and stretched, tired from an hour of filling out official papers on our grouchy old computer. After downing the last of me tea, I stood up, stretched again, and took a slow walk down the concrete runway between the pens. As I approached each cage, the occupant would snarl and bark, often charging the door as if to say, "Just let me get me teeth into you, you bugger!" I could only shake my head at the injustice of it all. It wasn't their fault they had never known affection, that their lives from day one had been a swirling mass of pain designed to make them vicious fighters who would attack anything, sometimes even their owners. Pit bull fighting is a nasty sport run by vile human beings who have little regard for life.

So what was this bulldog doing here? I stood outside his cage and studied him carefully. Unlike the others, he was a young dog. Did someone use him to train young pit bulls? Maybe that explained the scars across his face. He was a training dummy, a poor bloke who had the misfortune to wind up in a place where his life was expendable. He looked absolutely knackered. While all the other dogs had charged to the front snarling, he lay in a corner of the cage. His body language seemed to say "Just go away, will ya, and give a bloke a kip, eh?"[1]

---

[1] **Just let me sleep, will ya?**

I grasped the door and shook it. Immediately he was on his feet, barking loudly. But instead of lunging for me, he backed to the rear of the cage, his tail between his legs. His eyes that told me all I needed to know. They were not filled with anger and a desire to kill. They were filled with fear.

"It's okay, mate," I said quietly, "I'm not about hurting ya." I turned around and almost knocked Andy off his pins.

"Guess I'll do him next." He looked at me with a combination of sorrow and disgust. "You owe me a pint after work."

I put my hand on his and lowered the gun. "Go do the rest. Leave him alone. Understand?"

"You're kiddin', right? The old man'll have his knickers in a twist."

"No, he won't." I put my hand on his shoulder and led him away from the cage. "I'll go talk to him now." I turned back to the cage. "Andy, look at that bloke. There's something different about him. There's something there worth saving. I just know it."

That's what I told Tedford, the head of District B animal control. He looked at me as if I were gobsmacked.[2]

"So what do you want to do? Turn 'im loose?" He got up from behind the desk and came around to me. "Come on, John. You're off your trolley. He's a fightin' dog. He's a time bomb waiting to go off. You know that as well as any of us."

"I don't think so, sir." I returned his look, dead in the eyes. "He's not a killer. He's a scared dog who got his arse in a bad situation. I don't think he's much more than a real big pup someone thought they could use as a training dummy." I took a couple of steps closer and lowered my voice. "Come on, Teddie. At least give me a chance. The worst that happens is I get me arse

---

[2] **British slang for crazy**

chewed a bit, and that's nothing new."

Tedford stared me down for a few seconds, then with a deep sigh, returned to his desk. "Two conditions. One, if he so much as farts on someone, down he goes. And if you get seriously hurt, I didn't authorize you to do this. Got it?"

Sometime later I was made to think I perhaps should have listened to him.

I named him Bobby, after me late brother. I'll tell you something funny. I always thought me brother looked like a bulldog. He was a big guy with jowls, and his chin jutted out like a bulldog. But he and I were best mates and when he died, I went on a week-long bender that damn near killed me. I wasn't much good after that either. It was working with dogs that saved me life. I'd probably still be down in Liverpool, poppin' pills in some filthy flat if it wasn't for the kitten I found wandering down an alley. I took it to animal control and that's where I met Sheila. She cared for the kitten and she took care of me as well.

"You're a good-hearted lad, you know that?" I wasn't ready for that, so I kind of shuffled me feet and cleared me throat while she continued to wash the kitten with those gentle hands of hers. "I've seen what some people do to strays. You don't seem like that at all."

I took a liking to her and started showing up at the clinic just so I could be around her. It wasn't too long before she had me at work, first sloppin' out the cages, and then helping her with the larger dogs. I don't know if dogs have a soul, but working with them saved mine. When I first started working there I was still hurting for me brother – boozing and taking pills every weekend. It took a while, but Sheila was patient with me and finally, between her and the dogs, I somehow got cleaned up. Sheila said she was praying for me, but I didn't want to hear any of that God stuff. I just loved the animals and they gave me peace. I never figured God had much to do with it.

When Sheila got an offer to head up District A animal control she moved down to a little farm near Torrington and I followed along. Tedford – good old Teddie from District B – took me in as a favor to her. Somehow I've found a lot of peace comforting suffering animals. I'm not sure how that works, but I figured with Bobby I had a chance to pay it back to all the animals that had helped me over the years. I owed him at least that much – a chance. I know something about fear and pain.

We didn't get off to a good start. Bobby wouldn't let me get near him, no matter how soothingly I talked to him. I started with the only kindness I could think of – food. I told me mates in the district not to feed him so that I could be the only face he associated with this one small pleasure in his life. Any time I tried to get close to him he would slowly back into a corner with his tail between his legs and that scared look in his eyes. He never tried to lunge at me, but then again, I never got too close to him either. He's a well-built dog and powerful, and I gave him that respect.

I think I began to make progress the day I got the brilliant idea of cooking him up some bangers [3] for his dinner.

"You're bringing our good bangers to that dog?" Sheila needled me, trying to act offended, but smiling nonetheless. "Next thing you know you'll be bringing that dog home with you."

I reminded her that was the goal, kissed her goodbye, and smiled as I walked out the door.

"Here ya go, mate!"

---

[3] **Sausages**

I opened the door to his kennel and entered slowly. Bobby stared at me. The smell of bangers had his attention despite his fear. I approached him cautiously until he made a move backward. Stopping there, I took the lid off the container, kneeled down, and placed it on the floor. Bobby didn't move. I was hoping the bangers would bring him to approach me, but after ten minutes of staring at each other, it didn't appear to be working. I eased myself out the door and watched as he bounded over to the bangers and devoured them in a gulp. He looked at me and I wondered if that was a wee bit of a smile I saw or was it just the turn of his bulldog face?

We went on like this for a couple of weeks. Some days it was bangers, some days anything other than the dry dog food we give most of our patients. Bobby needed love and the only love I had to give him was real good food.

I must have been knackered the day it happened. I'm normally very aware of me surroundings in a kennel. A bloke has to be because you are working with animals in stress and they can be unpredictable. I had just entered Bobby's cage with a fresh baloney from the butcher over on Smythe Street when I turned me ankle on Bobby's water dish. The fall tossed me right at Bobby. I heard him growl, then a thousand hot irons dug into me face as he defended himself.

❀❀❀❀❀

"186 stitches, John." Teddie was standing at the foot of me cot in the emergency room. "I warned you, didn't I?"

He walked over to the side of the cot. "You're lucky he didn't tear your throat out, you damn fool." He paused. "I'm having him put down. It's over, John. You should thank God you're still alive."

I grabbed him as he turned to leave.

"Teddie, please! Just a fortnight more. I was getting closer to him every week." I tightened me grip on his wrist. "It's not his fault I scared him. Put yourself in his place. Anytime something lunged at him, it was trying to kill him." I lowered me voice to plead with Teddie. "If he meant to kill me, I'd be dead right now."

Teddie peeled me hand from his wrist and began to walk towards the door. "I know nothing about this. You hear me, John? Nothing! This was your decision and your fault." He stopped in the doorway and turned around, his eyes stern. "Right, John?"

I could only gratefully nod me head.

I don't know where I got the inspiration, but I had a night in the hospital to think and somewhere in the early hours of the morning I realized what I had to do. After she got the kids off to school, Sheila came back to bring me home. She listened wide-eyed as I explained me plan to her, then turned away in distress.

"Cor, love! I knew you were a little potty[4] when I met you, but this is ..." Her voice trailed off and she shook her head slowly from side to side. Turning back to me, she held a pocket mirror to me. "Johnny, look at your face." Tears ran down her cheeks. "I know the dog means a lot to you, but you have to give it up."

I took her hands in mine. "One more try. If this doesn't work, then I'll let go of him. Promise." I looked her in the eyes. "Aren't you the girl who said you love me because of how I treat animals? Do you really expect any less from me?"

I wonder if dogs think like we do. When I opened the door to the kennel and slowly slid in, Bobby cocked his head to one side. I could imagine him

---

[4] **Off one's rocker, not right in the head**

thinking, "*What the hell are you doing back here after the arse kickin' I gave you?*" I stood against the wall of the kennel, watching him carefully. After a minute, satisfied that I was not going for him, he settled back down with his head on his paws, eyeing me carefully.

I slowly eased down to the floor and lay on me back. That position means surrender when dogs fight. It's language that says to a dominant dog, "Okay. You win. Don't kill me, please." I was gambling that gentleness would win over authority.

Bobby's head turned to one side. He rose and cautiously walked to me. I held completely still, me right hand draped protectively across me neck, waiting for his next move. He lowered his head and sniffed me face, then softly licked the bandages on the right side before he lay down beside me. He put his big head against me chest and gave a deep sigh. I knew we had won.

Bobby stays in me office. I don't see the fear in his eyes anymore, but he's still a bit dodgy around strangers. Trust is coming slowly. When we go walking, people say we look like twins. I take that as a compliment.

I was walking by the old parish church in town last Sunday and for some strange reason I felt a strong desire to go inside. Mass was over and the church was dim except for a corner of brightly lit candles. I stood in the back for a while, terribly out of place. I hadn't felt a need for church since a kid. The only thing I ever remembered about church was that as a little bugger, I was scared by the sight of a bleeding man hanging on a giant cross. He was still up front, in the dim light behind the altar. I sat in a pew and stared for a while.

For the first time, those scars on His body made perfect sense.

Mu'izz

Iheard the sound as I was finishing with the last of 118 stitches in the face of the little girl the villagers had brought to me. A typical Afghani girl, big brown eyes and long dark hair, who was very scared but bravely letting me suture the damage that a suicide bomber had done earlier that day in the market of her town.

"Does that hurt?" I asked in my broken Arabic, my hand poised in midair between stitches. I wanted to be sure the Novocaine was still doing its job.

She gave me a shy smile, despite her fear, and shook her head a little. I put in the last stitch, tightened it up, and was gently washing away the dried blood when the blast shook my clinic. The girl screamed with fear. I instinctively covered her with my body and that is how I was when the Taliban militant burst through the door, slamming it open against the wall.

"Get up!"

I rose slowly to my feet and turned to face the voice. I guess all Middle Eastern men look pretty much the same to us Americans. He was man of medium height, young and well built, with a thick, short cut beard. His eyes radiated hatred. I was used to Taliban. I knew most of them in town, but this guy I had never seen before.

When they first came to the little village outside Gardez, they arrested me and spent a night interrogating me until the locals came and indignantly told them of the work I was doing in the village. There were a lot of threats and yelling and in the morning I was released – with an apology. I found that odd, given the intense dislike of the Taliban for anything American, but I thanked them and returned to work at the free clinic our organization had set up to treat refugees and victims of the war. I don't know what was said in the heat of the discussion – my Arabic is rudimentary at best – but I kept my mouth shut and a low profile for a while.

It was only after I stitched up one of their fighters that I was finally left completely alone. It seems to me that the Taliban either love you or hate you, and if you are their friend, you are friends for life. I wasn't taking sides in this war one way or the other. Some might call that treason, but my mission was strictly humanitarian, and if an injured man was brought to me, I treated him. Others could worry about his politics. For all I knew, it could have been a villager, since he wasn't carrying the usual brace of weaponry that they all seem to lug around. I'm not sympathetic to politics, just human suffering. That's why I became a surgeon. They brought me the wounded man and I sewed him up. Simple. Only later did I find out that he was Taliban.

"Another C.I.A. stooge," my captor sneered, in surprisingly good English.

"I'm Dr. Clyborne Ellsworthy. I'm not C.I.A." I eyed him up closely. "Is this your work?" I taunted him, turning aside to point to my little patient. "You proud of yourself, blowing up little girls?

I probably should have kept my mouth shut, but I was in a foul mood after seeing the carnage that had been brought to my clinic that morning. You want to blow yourself up – fine! Do it. Just don't take the innocent with you. The little girl had been the last straw for me in a long day of seeing innocent suffering and pain.

For my trouble I caught the butt of his rifle in my gut, then the last thing I remember was seeing stars as he brought it up and caught me in the face.

The first thing I smelled as I began to crawl out of the black fog of my unconsciousness was the distinct odor of urine. I winced a little as I tried to clear my head, and when I did, a sharp pain informed me that my nose was in bad shape. I placed my palms on the floor and lifted up slightly to take a look around. I was in a dim cell with one very small window high in the wall. Darkness was spreading through the room.

It took me a bit to make sense of it all, then I remembered my last interaction with the Taliban intruder. Who was this guy? I was a little scared, but very angry. Commander Safar had made it clear to everyone in town in no uncertain terms to leave me and the clinic alone. Surely this was some rogue and by the morning everything would be cleared up.

Seeing a cot against the wall, I crawled over to it on all fours and deposited myself on it. A quick manual examination of my nose verified what I already suspected. It was broken. I settled back on the cot and reached into my pocket. My Rosary was still there, along with the small prayer book I always carry with me. Couldn't be a better time to pray than this. I lay back on the cot, pulled the thin blanket over me against the oncoming evening cold, and began reciting the opening Creed. I don't remember if I got all the way through the Rosary before I fell back into a deep sleep.

"So...the infidel pig is awake!"

I had been awake for a couple of hours when I got his snarling greeting. Not exactly the greeting with which I wanted to start my day. And I was still upset that he had roughed me up. I let him know it.

"Thanks for breaking my nose, jerk." My tone was unmistakable. I should have learned from our encounter the day before, but I have a stubborn streak and a bad temper that keeps me in the confessional a lot.

With an angry grunt, he grabbed me, lifted me off the cot, and slammed me against the wall.

"C.I.A. scum! You will talk only to answer my questions." A fist slammed into my already sore ribs. "If you do not keep your infidel mouth shut, I will break more than your nose."

"Call Muhsin Ali Safar," I pleaded with him, my tone more respectful. The sooner I got free from this maniac, the better. In the meantime, I would eat humble pie before him if it would keep him calm. "He knows who I am."

"Muhsin is no longer here." His voice filled with disdain. "He is a pig – a traitor for allowing you to be here and not arresting you immediately. You may have tricked him, C.I.A. American, but you are not fooling me." He hit me again in the same spot. This time it really hurt. I gasped sharply. "I am Faruq Kassis. I am now station commander. Muhsin will be dealt with." He spat, then punched me again. "You will tell me your name, your rank in the C.I.A., and give me the names of your superiors."

That was when serious fear set in. I was used to living on edge, especially with American drones dropping randomly out of the sky, but this guy struck me as a borderline psychotic ready to hurt me badly. By the end of the day my worst fears were realized. He spent the day beating me, calling me a liar, and not listening to anything I said. No amount of reasoning could break through the hatred I saw in his face. He was determined that I was C.I.A. and that was that.

Looking back, I don't know how I made it through that first day. Perhaps it was the prayers to Our Lady I kept reciting under my breath as he beat on me. The rest of that first week was pretty much the same. He would burst in, screaming curses against Bush, the USA, and everything American, then proceed to slap me around a little before beginning his questioning routine. When I insisted that I was not C.I.A. and told him to check with the villagers, he would become enraged, and scream out something in Arabic. Two other men, mean looking guys with AK-47's, would show up and he would put down his gun and light into me with both hands.

By the end of the week, I had a number of ugly looking hematomas, at least two broken ribs that I could feel, and was struggling to remember Our Lord's words about praying for your enemies and doing good to those who despitefully use you. All day I would get angrier and angrier at his injustice toward me. I would fantasize about slamming him against the wall and smacking him around. I'm six feet four and played football at Duke, but size is no match for an AK- 47. At night, I would pray for the strength to forgive this man. Often I thought of the martyrs of the faith and asked for their intercession. Somehow when I woke in the morning, facing another day of his brutality, I felt strong enough to endure it. By the end of each day I was begging God to let me die.

I wondered how I would be able to show kindness to him in order to obey Our Lord's command. The opportunity came before I had to endure another week's worth of beatings.

❀❀❀❀❀

"American pig!" Faruq burst through the door, screaming obscenities at me. "Look what you have done!" He was clutching a large German Shepherd to his chest. There was blood all over his clothes. The dog had a sizeable wound in its side and blood was seeping out onto Faraq.

My words came before I thought about them. "Let me help you." He paused and glared at me. I put my hand on my cot. " Put the dog down and I will help you."

I will never forget the look he gave me. His face suddenly changed to fear and sorrow. He was silent, but his eyes were pleading.

"Do you have my medical bag?" He stared at me in puzzlement. "A black bag with medical instruments in it." I could see the confusion in his eyes as he struggling to remember if he had seen it. "If you want your dog to live, get me that bag – now! Find it!"

He was gone a long time. I found out later he went all the way back to the clinic to retrieve it. Somehow, in God's mercy, the dog stayed alive. It was a nasty wound, about fifty centimeters long. The deepest part ran along his abdominal cavity, exposing the intestines, which were trying to work their way out. I held the dog on his side and pushed against the wound with a dirty towel I had been using to wash my face. With my free hand I stroked the dog's head. Despite his pain, he managed to turn his head and lick my hand.

When Faruq returned with the bag, I quickly located my scissors and removed as much hair as I could. Then I cleaned the wound down to the bare skin with a couple of razors before examining the wound more closely. The intestines appeared to be intact, but I wanted to make sure. No sense in sewing up the dog, then have him die from peritonitis.

As I gently eased the intestine out of the body, Faruq gave a gasp and cried out that I was killing him, but he made no move towards me. Whatever had done this had sliced the skin as if a razor had run over it. Once I was satisfied there was no internal damage, I poured alcohol on the wound and began to suture. It was the best I could offer under those circumstances. The dog was still conscious enough to whimper in pain. I paused to stroke his head.

"I know, boy. I'm sorry. It's the best I can do for you now." I went back to my stitching. When I finished, I turned to Faruq. "He has to stay here. If you try to move him, the stitches will break, his insides will come out, and he will die."

"If he dies, I will kill you."

I don't even know what I was thinking at that moment. I had endured a week of his threats and beatings and was probably just tired of it all. I slowly rose to my feet and tore the rags of my shirt from my body, exposing the mass of purple bruises and swollen knots where my ribs were broken.

"Why don't you just do it now and get it over with? You would be doing me a favor." I wasn't screaming or mad. My voice was even and my tone said very simply. *"You want to do it, then let's do it and get it over with."* At that point, I honestly didn't care any more.

Faruq stared at my body for a few seconds, then looked at his dog, back to me, then at his dog again. A funny look came over his face, his jaw muscles tensed and his eyes clouded with realization, confusion, and guilt. He made a sudden guttural noise and ran out the still open door, his hands pressed to the sides of his head.

He was back early the next morning. In his hands was a large tray, piled with food and a tall glass of iced tea. Over his left arm were draped a clean shirt and pants. He placed the tray in front of me and without a word made a sweeping gesture toward it with his left hand.

I took a few sips of the tea, trying to get my stomach primed for some food. The last week's rations had been meager at best. I knew better than to try to stuff myself immediately, despite the wonderful smell coming from the tray. I broke off a small piece Zattar Bread and placed some Grilled Halloumi Cheese and Greek olives on it and set it by the tray. My stomach growled with anticipation.

"Eat." Faruq urged me. I turned my attention to the new clothes. They were freshly washed and smelled of soap. They had that wonderful soft feel of freshly cleaned clothing, a pleasure against my skin as I changed. "Please!" He urged again.

I nodded and put the piece I had set aside in my mouth. Delicious! I wanted to shovel it all in as fast as I could, but I knew better. "Such a beautiful dog. But dogs are unclean for Muslims. How is that you have a dog?"

There was a long silence. He turned to stare at the dog, his eyes filled with concern. "He is not moving." He made a motion with his hands to me, his eyes seeking reassurance.

"I found some morphine in my bag and I gave him a little to keep him still. He can't be up and running around or he will tear out his stitches." I pointed to the couch where the dog still lay. "Why don't you go over there and comfort him?"

Faruq went over to the cot, put his arms around the dog and gently buried his face in the fur of the neck. He stayed that way for a long time. Finally he rose from sitting next to his dog himself up and answered my question.

"I have had him since a puppy." Faruq paused and drew a deep breath, then let it out slowly, filled with emotion. "His name is Mu'izz." He leaned against the wall and regarded me with interest. "I am surprised you know about dogs and Muslims."

Unable to continue he stood up, walked over to the window of the cell, and stared out. Several minutes passed. I moved over to Mu'izz to check on him. Faruq seemed torn between letting his emotions out and maintaining his dignity before the American. Emotions finally won. When he turned back to me there were tears on his cheeks.

"My mother found him in the street and brought him home for me. It was after my brother was killed by American soldiers. Perhaps she thought that he would make me forget. The mullah at our mosque gave us permission to keep him for security, but he never goes inside my house." He kicked the dirt in the cell, then turned to pound his fist against the wall. "Jibran was walking home from school and the soldiers shot him. He wasn't doing anything."

I looked down at the floor, then away. "I'm sorry." At first I didn't know if he heard me. My voice was low with shame that our soldiers would do such a thing. But he heard. It was the wrong time to offer apologies.

"Sorry?" He screamed. "Sorry?" His fists clenched. "My whole family is gone now! They are all gone! Killed by American bombs and American soldiers!" He strode over to where I was kneeling by Mu'izz, checking his stitches while I stroked his head. Faruq's face was alive, his eyes wide, his mouth open. He clenched his hands into fists and yelled at me again, his face close to mine, his eyes wide with emotion. His voice was filled with confusion.

"I want to be mad at you." I expected him to strike me, but instead he turned on his feet and began rapidly pacing the cell. "I hate you Americans."

"I didn't do it," I responded in a low, even voice.

"I want to be mad at you."

"Be mad at my country. Be mad at men who kill innocent people."

"You are American!"

"Faruq, I didn't do it." I watched him as he continued to pace back and forth. "There is nothing I can say that will make you feel better. I don't know what to say. I don't know what to tell you. You are right to be angry."

"I do not understand."

"I don't understand it either. The hate. The lies. I can't stand seeing it every day."

"No." He whipped around to face me. "I do not understand why you are not mad at me. Why do you not hate me after what I have done to you?" His voice filled with confusion. "Why did you not kill Mu'izz to get even?"

I took a few seconds to think of my response before I gave it. "Because my God does not allow me the luxury of hate. Jesus told us to love our enemies."

"You are a Christian?" Reflexively he spat on the floor. "You believe in three gods like the other idol worshipers!" Disgust filled his voice.

"No. There is only one God."

What happened next surprised me. Somehow my comment set off a very lively discussion. I was careful not to say anything about The Prophet. Just getting Faruq to talk politely with me about religion was a huge victory, and I didn't want to lose it. I had no idea where this was going, but my sense as a Christian told me to trust God wherever it went. We spent an hour talking about the concept of the Trinity while I nibbled at the food he had brought me. At the end of the hour, half the tray was gone and I was feeling a lot better with some food in my stomach.

"You are good at explaining your religion, but I still cannot believe in your three god one god." He waved his hand dismissively. "I think you Christians are all crazy." But there was a hint of a smile on his face when he said it.

"Does Allah love?"

"Yes. Of course. Allah loves. Allah is merciful and Allah loves."

"Who did He love before He created any of this?"

"There was no need to love because there was no one."

"Then Allah could not love because there was no one." I reached for another small bite of the Zattar bread. "Look, Faruq. Here is the difference. Christians believe that God *is* love. Not just that He chooses to love, but that He *is* love. If one chooses to love, one can choose to hate. But if God *is* love, then all He can do is to love. And that means to be love there had to be Someone for Him to love." I paused to pop more bread into my mouth before I continued. "If Allah had never created anyone, He would still be love, and would have to have another to love. Without another, He couldn't be love."

Faruq stared at me as I slowly chewed and sucked on the delicious morsel in my mouth. Finally he rose and went over to Mu'izz. Kneeling beside the dog, he stoked his pet's head for several minutes. His face was a map of emotions. Before he walked out the door, he turned to me.

"Thank you. I do not know if Mu'izz will live, but thank you for all you have done."

I did not know either, but I prayed a full Rosary that night, both for Mu'izz and for Faruq.

The beatings stopped. Mu'izz slowly recovered. To this day I believe it was a miracle. I don't know how much blood he lost, but it looked like a lot, and I can't figure out how he did so well without a transfusion. I kept him sedated for a week, with just enough morphine to make him groggy but not to knock him out. That kept him from trying to get up and run around. I had a feeling that he was a frisky dog and I was right. The day I weaned him off the morphine, he arose, shook himself thoroughly, and ran over to Faruq to cover him in loving doggie kisses. It was a joyful reunion, one that got me a bit misty eyed. After watching them for several minutes, I popped my question on Faruq.

"Do I get to return to my clinic now?"

The look I got from him all but said, *"What are you, nuts?"* Turning to Mu'izz, he barked out a command in Arabic. The dog immediately sat down, staring up lovingly at his master.

"You crazy American." He sighed and turned to look out the little window of my cell. "I don't believe anymore that you are C.I.A., but it is not that easy." When he turned back to me, his lips were tight. "I told unit commander Hamid you are C.I.A. and I would break you to get information. He has been demanding where my information is all this week." He turned back to the window. "I cannot put him off much longer. And I certainly cannot just let you go. He will find you and probably kill you."

"Why don't you just tell him that you found out I'm not C.I.A.?"

"You do not know Taliban, do you?" He walked over to where I was sitting and pulled up a chair to sit down. "It is not that easy."

"What kind of commander doesn't believe his men?"

"One who believes any American in Afghanistan is either an American soldier or a C.I.A. spy. There's no other reason for an American to be in this area." He stared into my eyes. "Well, is there?"

I suddenly understood. He was right. A recent news story had revealed that a so-called "medical team" giving out polio vaccines in Pakistan had been C.I.A. operatives trying to get information. Not only had it ruined any future attempts by real medical teams to vaccinate children, it had been the cause of nine deaths in reprisal – deaths of legitimate medical workers who were in the wrong place at the wrong time. Now I was the one in the wrong place at the wrong time. I was about to find out just how wrong.

Two days later, in the early morning, Faruq came flying awkwardly through the door of the cell. He was followed by the large Taliban who had pushed him into my cell. There was an angry exchange of words between the two, then Faruq turned to me.

"Commander Hamid does not speak English, so I can talk freely. Give me something I can tell him." Faruq's eyes were pleading. "If you do not give me information, he says he is going to shoot you." He balled his left hand into a fist. His eyes told me he was sorry for what he had to do.

He started on the ribs on my right side, the ones that weren't broken. He was good at making the punches look hard, but keeping them from really hurting. Every time he hit me I let out a gasp and groaned. If Faruq was going to try to save my life, I was going to help him as best I could.

He was winding up for another shot when the Taliban commander pushed him aside roughly, balled up his fist, and slugged me right on my broken ribs. I let out a scream and dropped to the floor in agony.

The commander turned to Faruq and there was another angry exchange in Arabic. I was gasping for air when Hamid grabbed me and lifted me to my feet. Lord, was he strong! He pulled up my dead weight as if he were a child lifting a toy.

"Not C.I.A." I gasped, begging. "Oh, God, please." I was shaking my head in denial and kept yelling I was not C.I.A.

The last thing I remember clearly was him winding up for another punch and then all hell broke loose. I heard voices yelling and cursing in English. Gunfire, close and loud, made my ears ring. Hamid's eyes got real wide, then he dropped me and slumped to the ground. Looking up in pain I saw the faces of armed men in American Army combat fatigues.

Outside the cell I could hear more gunfire and screaming. An older man with a red medical cross on his helmet dragged me to the side of the cell and propped me up. Four other soldiers were securing the area, one at the door, one looking out the window in quick glances, and the other two holding their weapons at ready. I could hardly breathe and could feel my ribs clicking with every painful breath I took.

"It's okay, sir. We're going to get you out of here."

"Faruq!" My head was clearing. "Where's Faruq?" I leaned forward, trying to see past the two soldiers who were guarding me. I could see a pair of feet beyond the one soldier, and I immediately recognized the worn shoes on them. It was Faruq. I pushed the medic away and scrambled on all fours to get to him, yelling his name.

He was still alive when I turned him over. He opened one eye slowly, his lips pulled back in an ironic smile.

"And now they have killed us all." He struggled for his breath, then opened both eyes and looked directly into mine. "I guess we don't get to talk about your crazy one god in three gods anymore." There was a pause and he found my hand and grasped it. "You are a good man, Dr. Clyborne Ellsworthy. Pray to your one god in three gods for me when I am dead."

Faruq's eyes rolled back in his head and he gave a last rattling sigh. I screamed his name and began CPR on him. The soldiers probably thought I had lost my mind. I kept it up for fifteen minutes, yelling at him not to die and begging God to spare his life, until finally the medic gently pulled me away.

"He's gone, sir. You can't bring him back."

The fighting lasted for another hour. I hadn't realized I was at a Taliban compound where there were a number of high level commanders assembled. When the fighting stopped the soldiers picked up their gear and we headed out of the compound. The Army guys wanted to put me on a chopper and get me out of there, but I wasn't leaving until I took care of some unfinished business. We got into a furious argument until I finally shoved the corporal holding on to me and started to walk towards the village. My ribs were aching, but I was not leaving until I got what I wanted. I heard the first sergeant order two men to accompany me and I turned and waved them off.

"Don't. You'll get yourself shot. Stay here till I return. The people in this village know me and they won't hurt me. You – they will kill on sight." I returned an hour later with Mu'izz on a rope I had made into a leash. I found him waiting for Faruq in the ruins of the house where they lived.

When he saw the chopper and the soldiers, he stopped and wouldn't go any further. No amount of coaxing could make him come with me. When I was going to fetch him I had thought of this possibility and I had stopped at my clinic and had gotten a fresh vial of morphine from the safe. I put Mu'izz to sleep and the Army guys loaded him into the chopper and we got out of there. On the ride home I told them the story of Faruq and Mu'izz and Faruq's family. They were quiet after I finished. I think one of them might have been crying.

It's been a year since all that took place. It has taken a lot of love and care, but Mu'izz has finally adapted to my family and his new surroundings. Every so often for the first few months I would find him pacing around the yard, sniffing the air and whining. I knew he was looking for Faruq and wondering where his beloved master could be. I think it took me longer to get over those events than it did him. I was depressed for months, and often when I thought of Faruq I would break down and weep.

I pray everyday for the repose of his soul. The Catholic Catechism teaches us that there is such a thing as the "baptism of desire." That is to say, if a soul wishes to be baptized but dies before he or she can be baptized, God recognizes that longing and considers it to be as if the person did enter the waters of Baptism.

I hold that hope in my heart for Faruq. I hold it very tightly.

FLAT BOTTOM
BILLY

I remember the events as if it were yesterday. It was 1994 and I was a couple of years out of college and working as a teaching assistant at St. Alphonsus Liguori High School.

There are people who are plain in our school and then there was Billy. He was a kind of mound of flesh on two stubby legs. His clothes never really fit him correctly and seemed eternally wrinkled. His hair hung past his shoulders in long, greasy waves, untouched by a comb or brush.

Billy had small, dark eyes which were set deeply into a round pie plate of a face and peered out at the world from under bushy eyebrows. His face was framed by two large ears standing out from the sides of his head, almost as if waving for attention.

His face was pock marked – scarred would actually be a more accurate description – from a long time teenage bout with a particularly vicious case of acne. I suppose that was why he never shaved. No razor would have been able to completely clean off the whiskers, given the craggy state of his face. Because of the acne, what little beard he was able to grow was sparse and straggly.

The most prominent feature on this mask of a face was his nose. It was large and red, rough and bulbous, the kind of nose that normally would indicate the owner to be a serious alcoholic – except that Billy didn't drink. It was one of many features of this poor kid which offered a target for serious abuse.

Underneath the nose was a mouth that almost never smiled. When Billy did, he revealed a mouthful of nasty looking teeth. It was painful to observe this serious need of proper hygiene. The whole effect from top to bottom was to make one think of a hobo, a guy who had spent his life riding the rails and eating out of cold cans of beans.

Why was he called "Flat Bottom Billy?"

It was because of his bottom – or actually, his lack of one. He simply had no butt. He wore loose fitting jeans or overalls that dropped straight down and gave no indication of gluteus maximus. It was weird looking the way his pants fit him, and the class clowns quickly picked up on it when he first entered high school. Like I said, he was just a large flesh pudding of a boy, an overweight body with a terribly unattractive face. He showed up in the morning, shuffled from class to class, and disappeared without a word as soon as the last bell rang.

He never showed up for gym class and the principal couldn't make him. On day one in the ninth grade, after he skipped gym, Principal Pochino sat him down in his office and told him that he would go or face suspension and a fine. Billy simply refused to comply with the order.

A week after a note was sent to his house informing his mother that either he attend class or she would be fined, she filed a formal complaint with the school district, citing some obscure law on the books about bullying. This was followed up by a tersely worded letter from a local lawyer in which said lawyer stated that he would be all too happy to take the principal to court and "take you down a notch or two from your imperious seat of persecution of this poor boy." After a half an hour's deliberation, the school board decided they had bigger fish to fry than to get involved in a case that would only bring discredit upon them. They voted to drop the whole matter and Billy was free of that torment. It was a small victory in a life of misery.

If Billy was the most unattractive kid in the school, Alex Turner was, without a doubt, the best looking. I used to wonder – before the incident last took place – why it is that God seems to give so much to some and so little to others. If fate had been chinchy with Billy, she made up for it in spades with Alex.

Alex was a teenage girl's dream date, a kid who had everything going for him. He was six-foot four with movie star good looks. The young man had it all – wavy blonde hair, nice complexion, a winning smile, perfect teeth, and a body sculpted by a couple of years of faithful attendance at the local gym. Add to all these physical attributes the ability to ace his exams, three years of lettering on the varsity baseball and football teams, and a full ride to Cal State in the coming year, and there you have a kid who had his whole life sitting in front of him shouting "Come and get it!" Billy and Alex were two incredible contrasts walking through the halls of the same building every day.

Their contrast was never more clearly defined than during lunchtime. Billy's usual place was the last table in the dining room where he would sit by himself and slowly eat his lunch. Alex would hold court at the center table where he could regale his friends and adoring teenage girls with tales of what he had done the past weekend. The only time they ever came close to interacting was when Billy would shuffle by Alex's table and Alex would have something cruel to say about Billy's appearance. Then the whole table would have a good laugh at Billy's expense and they would turn to their lunch while Billy quietly continued over to his usual seat in the back.

I was sitting in the lunchroom one day, staring out the window, when a thought came to me. I had plans for that night, and the thought struck me *"What does a boy like Billy do with his weekends? Where does he spend his free time?"* Did he have some small group of friends unknown to the rest of the world at St. Alphonsus Liguori? Or did he while away his weekends with a joystick in his hands and a bag of chips on the chair between his legs? For some reason, the thought of him spending his time alone with a video game as his only companionship suddenly seemed a very sad and lonely thing to me. It was odd, for I had never given Billy a second thought since the day a year ago when I started as a teacher's assistant. Now I was pushed by a deep curiosity to know more about this sad individual who I saw everyday but did not know.

He looked up as I approached the table.

"Hello. You mind if I borrow the salt? There doesn't seem to be any at my table."

Come on. I mean, what was I going to say? *"You look lonely sitting over here. Would you like company?"* That would be just a little too awkward. As he pushed the salt shaker towards me with the back of his hand, I noticed a book lying beside his lunch tray. Perfect!

"Oh, that's interesting. What's the book about?"

Billy stared at me for a second, his head tilted to one side, his eyes filled with a combination of confusion and distrust. At first I thought he would just ignore me and return to his lunch. Then he straightened up his head and replied. "You probably wouldn't be interested in it. Just a bunch of specs for my hobby."

I had to work at hearing him over the noise of the cafeteria. His voice was withdrawn and quiet, but the words were clear and I understood what he said. I took a second and closer look at the cover. It appeared to be some sort of tool catalog. There were miniature files, small lathes, Dremel motors, and an assortment of other items that are generally used in metal working.

"That doesn't look like specs to me," I opined. "It looks more like a variable speed Dremel tool, five thousand to twenty-five thousand RPMS with an assortment of tools for a locking collet." I was lucky. I happen to have one just like it in my workshop at home. Handy little tool. Especially for keeping a conversation going at that moment.

"That's right," Billy offered firmly. "How do you know that?" We spent the next half hour talking about tools and our respective hobbies. Billy enthused about working with metal and creating statues and chess sets. I couldn't imagine his stubby fingers being able to create much more than a rudimentary mess, but at the same time, it was amazing to see this shy kid come out of his shell and glowingly talk about his hobby.

The school bells rang, signifying the end of lunch. "Would you like to see some of my work?"

How was I going to say no? I agreed to meet Billy at lunch the next day and look at his creations. As we parted, I made a mental note to practice looking amazed and appreciative. I could have saved myself the trouble.

Billy placed a small canvas bag on the table between us and brought out the pieces he wanted to share with me. I was stunned by what I saw. Each piece was approximately four inches in height and exquisitely detailed. They must have been from the chess set he had been discussing with me the day before. There were two small men, dressed in what appeared to be Medieval peasant garb, a knight upon a horse, and a bishop with his crosier. Standing slightly taller was a very regal looking king, complete with beard and crown.

As he arranged them in a line on the table, I leaned in for a closer examination. These were not quickly done pieces. Each face had incredible detail. In a working area the size of a quarter, Billy had created eyebrows, ears, eyes, nose and mouth with precise features. The king's crown was emblazoned with small crosses. Within the curl of the bishop's crosier was a tiny cross. On his bishops mitre were engraved tiny crosses and intricate scroll work. For a second, I was at a loss for words.

"How in the world do you do this?"

A small smile played at the edge of his mouth. "I just do it. I've.....well, I've always liked doing this sort of thing. It just kind of comes naturally to me."

"Well, what do we have here? Little dollies?" I looked up to the strange and menacing voice. It was Alex. There was a mean smile on his face, his eyes filled with contempt. "You boys playing with dolls now?"

"Not dolls, Alex," I replied evenly. "Look at them. Billy makes these. Look at the work he's done here."

Alex paused for a second, as if my words had taken momentary root in his mind, then with a flick of his wrist, swept the figures from the table to the floor. "Ahhhhh, who cares?" He turned to walk away.

"Hey, Alex." I stood up slowly from the table as he turned around. "You need to pick those up and put them back where you found them." His eyes narrowed coldly. I stared right back at him. "I'm not asking you, Alex. I'm telling you."

I don't know if he forgot I am a teacher's assistant because I was almost his age at that time, or if he was just caught up in his need to be Mr. Big Shot in the lunchroom, but his next move set the table for me. Taking a quick stride to within three feet of me, he reached out and shoved me.

"You gonna make me?"

It was a typical piece of teenage posturing, a move designed to establish, by means of back and forth shoving between two guys, who is highest in the pecking order. Eventually the shoving will either die down or a fight will ensue to determine who wins. What Alex didn't know – in fact, what no one knew because I had kept it to myself – was that I have been studying multiple forms of martial arts for seventeen years. As a youngster, I got tired of being the little kid that all the bullies used as a target for life's frustrations. That stopped in junior high after I took a smart aleck who was shoving me around and put his face through a plate glass window. I didn't mean to do that. I had forgotten the window was behind me, but it accomplished what it needed to accomplish. I was left alone after that.

The cafeteria slowly grew silent as the whole scene began to play out. Alex loomed over me, his six-foot four frame dwarfing me by almost a foot. Cursing me, he made a move to shove me again. I instinctively responded with a knife edge block. With my free hand I grasped his wrist and turning into him, flipped him neatly over my shoulder. He landed with a satisfying thud on the hard linoleum of the cafeteria. Before he could get up, my fist found his nose. He lay stunned for a second, then began moan.

"Yeah. Hurts being on the other end, don't it?" I guess it wasn't particularly nice of me, but I like to rub it in when a bully gets his comeuppance. I knelt down beside him. "You take a moment to get your breath back, then when you feel like it, get up and put those statues back on the table. And while you are at it, give Billy an apology."

Alex glared at me. He was beaten, but still defiant. There was not a word from him. He slowly raised himself to his elbows, then reached up to wipe the blood trickling from his nose.

"You're gonna pay for this," he growled.

"Fine. You wanna dance? Let's go outside right now and dance." Then I noticed he was looking beyond me. I stood and turned to see two of his football buddies standing a few feet away. The whole cafeteria had fallen silent, the only noise being the clanking of silverware and plates from the kitchen. I had a pretty good sense of what they were thinking.

"Guys, don't get involved in this. This is between Alex and me."

Dave Morris, the bigger of the two, made a sudden rush for me and found himself flying through the air. The nice part about Ju Jitsu is that you use the size and momentum of your opponent against him. The bigger the opponent, the more you have to use, and this kid had a lot of both. I must have tossed him a good five feet. I have to hand it to him though, he landed like a cat and sprang back up for more. Instinctively I did a defensive back kick. My foot found its target and the second kid, who had decided to rush me when my back was turned, crumpled to the ground.

As Dave charged me I stepped aside and delivered a roundhouse kick to his thigh. I was finished being Mr. Nice Guy. The kick was full force and was designed to do one thing – break his leg. My shin contacted his thigh just as he put all his weight on it. It was like breaking a two by four in class. He dropped and began to scream.

"Damn, Dave!" My adrenalin was pumping and I screamed at him in anger. "You're as stupid as you are big! I told you not to screw with me!" I took out my cell phone and dialed 911. He was going to need to go to the emergency room. I tried to calm down as I told the operator on the other end what had happened and then turned back to Dave. "Lie still. You've got a broken femur and if it cuts your artery, you will bleed to death before they get here." He looked at me, his eyes filling with fear as he tried to remain still despite the pain.

I heard Principle Pochino's voice in the background, then a chorus of other voices. He was yelling at me, I was trying to concentrate on keeping Dave calm, and in the meantime, Alex got up and began to wail about how I had jumped him and I should be kicked out of school and so on and so forth. It was utter chaos. Kids were taking Alex's side and I heard a couple of threats. The appearance of the ambulance crew only made matters worse. Fortunately, they were accompanied by a couple of county policemen who finally got everything settled down, hustled the kids out of the cafeteria, and then began to question me in an unfriendly way.

Since I didn't have a mark on me, the police were taking Alex's word that I had jumped him for no reason at all. It didn't help that a little group of Alex worshipers meandered back into the cafeteria and began to support Alex's bogus charges. One of the policemen finally turned his attention to them and informed them in no uncertain terms that they could either leave or face arrest for interfering with their investigation. He appeared to be about as tired and annoyed by them as I was.

Only after the police took my suggestion and watched the videos from the cafeteria security cameras did they agree with me it had been self-defense. I declined to press charges against Alex, since he had already had enough punishment for the day. He was probably going to get suspended from school for attacking a teacher's assistant, which was fine with me. The whole thing needed to quiet down, but I had a bad sense Alex was not going to let it die.

I was right – and in a way that I have come to very much regret over the years.

❀❀❀❀❀

I wouldn't say that Billy and I became close buddies after the incident, but we did keep in touch at the cafeteria. I went over to his house once at his invitation. I was actually interested in how this awkward lump of a kid could create such beautiful work. What I found was not what I expected.

I thought I would find a messy workshop in the basement of a dingy house. What I found was a neat little bungalow on the poorer side of town. The lawn and bushes were nicely trimmed, with a recent paint job and cheery, clean windows. It stood out in contrast to the other run down and sad buildings on his block.

Billy did have a basement workshop. By the time he took me down the steps and into the small basement filled with rows of tools hanging on pegboards, I was not surprised to see that everything had a place and there was a place for everything. It was almost comical, since my workshop is constantly in need of cleaning and organization. Yet here was this unkempt mound of a boy proudly showing me each of his creations and describing in detail the tools he hung with such care on the pegboard behind his workbench. I pulled up a stool and watched him work on his latest creation, a magnificent lion's head.

"I'm just finishing this up," he intoned, concentrating on the movement of his Dremel as the blade on it cut separations into the hair of the lion's mane. I marveled at how his pudgy fingers so dexterously moved the head about and how easily he maneuvered the Dremel tool over the surface of the metal. "Actually, this was a pretty easy piece." He blew some filings off the head, turned it back and forth inspecting it, then handed it to me. "What do you think?"

"I think you are a very talented guy," I mused, running my fingers over the still warm metal. "Have you ever thought about selling your work?"

"I do sell my stuff. Online mostly. And sometimes at shows, although I don't really like to go to shows because everyone wants to beat you down on price." He hung the Dremel tool on a peg and turned to me. "There's no dickering online. People pay the price I ask."

"Billy, everything here is so neat and orderly. Yet you come to school looking..."

"Like a hobo?" he finished for me. "I know." He turned to face me. "Mr. Cameron, look at me. Do you think anything is going to change this face? This body? Nice clothes? Good pair of shoes?" His voice was quiet and factual. But more than that, I heard something else in his voice. He was a young man who had come to terms with who he was and had accepted it. "I guess I just don't much care." He gave me an odd look. "That would be like trying to make a silk purse out of a sow's ear, wouldn't it?"

"But why not?" I was puzzled. "You care about this part of your life. Look at how neat your wonderful little workshop is. Why not care about what you present to people?" I reached over to pick up a delicately wrought fairy. "You wouldn't take this to sell at show unless it was perfect, would you? And why? Because it's a reflection of you, a reflection of something that you are rightly proud of – your talent. Why not take pride in how people see you?"

"Why? So I can get a bunch of false friends like Alex has? People who would be my buddy if I was tall and handsome and could throw a football for touchdowns?" His voice had a sudden edge to it. He slid off his seat and started up the steps, still holding the lion's head in his hands. "I'll show you out. I've got some things to do." There was no mistaking the tone in his voice. There was no malice in it, but I had hit a nerve – one I hadn't meant to hit. At the top of the steps he turned to me and slowly held his hands out.

"I want you to have this. I've been making this for you." I was caught by surprise and for a moment couldn't respond. It was an offer of friendship and that after I had just badly stepped his feelings.

"Thanks." I took the lion from him. "Billy, look....I'm sorry if I said anything to hurt your feelings."

He sighed. The air was tense with silence. Finally I thanked him again and went out the door. I would have done better to have kept my questions to myself. Why did I have to be so nosy about something that was so clearly none of my business?

After a few quiet weeks I had begun to think that the whole incident in the cafeteria had blown over. Things were pretty much back to normal, except that Alex no longer had anything to say to Billy when he was near him. He left Billy alone, which was fine with me, although I saw a look in his eyes that I didn't care for. I had a bad feeling that Alex was blaming Billy for the embarrassment of getting his ass whupped in public and was thinking of ways he could get revenge.

I was not wrong. I regret that I didn't have the courage to go talk to him. Perhaps if I had sat down with Alex and had a man-to-man with him, the incident would have never happened.

❁❁❁❁❁

I was in the cafeteria eating when I heard a commotion over where Alex could normally be found with his retinue. There were loud voices, a single voice cried out "NO!" and then two girls began to shriek and wail. I put my sandwich on the tray and walked quickly to the table.

"What is it? What's happened?"

"Alex is in the hospital!" The cafeteria had become quiet. "He's badly burned." One of the girls to my side began to wail. "He's going to die!"

"It's that stupid Flat Bottom Billy's fault," chimed in a voice from behind me.

"What?" I exclaimed. "What do you mean? How was Billy part of this?"

"Billy's house burned down."

"And....?"

Suddenly there was embarrassing quiet, which told me Alex was somehow in Billy's house when he had no reason to be there.

"What happened? Where's Billy? Is he okay?"

"Awww, who the hell cares?" It was Farner Courman, one of Alex's close friends from the football team. I stared at the kid, trying to resist the urge to punch him right in his smart-ass nose. Lord have mercy, how do people become that cruel and uncaring, especially in a Catholic high school? I shoved him hard as I brushed past him and ran out to my car.

I found Billy still in the ER at the hospital. His arms were covered in thick bandages and the left side of his head was swathed in white. He was sedated, but he managed a soft greeting to me when I entered his room.

"Can you talk?" When he nodded, I continued. "What happened?"

Billy told me that Alex had broken into his house with a two liter bottle filled with gasoline. He had gone down to Billy's workshop and spread it generously over the entire area. What he was not expecting was for Billy to be home from school that day with a nasty cold. They met just as Alex stepped through the basement door, trailing gasoline into the living room as a fuse for his planned destruction of Billy's workshop.

The sudden encounter startled him and in his confusion he dropped the bottle, still half filled with gasoline. It rolled back down the stairs into the basement, which was probably what saved his life. The doctors told me later that if the explosion had caught the bottle of gasoline still in Alex's hand, there wouldn't have been enough left of him to bury in a sardine can. It would have killed Billy as well.

As it happened, the fumes from the gasoline were at just the right percentage to ignite when the old furnace in the basement suddenly clicked on. A massive explosion roared up the stairs and through the open door, the force of it throwing Billy through the plate glass of the patio doors behind him. The glass ripped his arms and the flames took their toll on his left side.

Alex was lifted off his feet and thrown into the brick fireplace next to the patio doors. He lay unconscious on the living room floor as the flames roared across the ceiling and began to devour the house. Billy lay outside, conscious but stunned, unaware of the second and third degree burns on his face and arms.

When the fire company arrived, they found Billy sitting against a tree, breathing heavily and in pain. Alex's limp body was lying at his feet. From the marks on the patio and the ground, Fire Chief Morton told me later he figured Billy went back into the blazing house, found Alex, and dragged him to safety. For some reason, Billy didn't mention that to me as we were talking.

Both boys had nasty burns, but Alex by far got the worst of it. I came back a week later to check in on both of them and that was when I really took a good look at the damage caused by the explosion. A couple of doctors and a nurse were changing the dressing on his burns when I walked in. They chased me out of the room, and not too politely, but not before I got a good look.

The entire left side of Alex's face was destroyed. The fire had ravaged his head from the crown of his head to the top of his shoulder. I was outside his room when I heard him cry out in pain. Debriding burns is terribly painful, yet it must be done or the burn site will become infected. I hate to admit it, but I was struggling with my own feelings about Alex. May the Lord forgive me, there was a part of me that honestly felt he got exactly what he deserved for his mean spirited attempt at revenge. But then I remembered that we are supposed to pray for our enemies and those who are ...well, who are just outright jerks like Alex.

When I went into Billy's room, I found him praying the Rosary. I couldn't hear him pray, but I could see him quietly fingering a bead for each Hail Mary. His eyes were closed and he looked almost relaxed, with a very serene expression on his face. When he came to the end of the decade he was praying, I broke in.

"Mind if I join you?"

Billy opened his eyes slowly and took a long, deep breath, letting it out in kind of a yawn. He offered me a little smile and nodded his head. We finished the next two decades together and recited the closing prayers. When we came to the Memorare, he very quietly reduced me to tears with his petition.

"Blessed Virgin Mary, help me to forgive Alex for what he did to me. And please help Alex to get better."

I had to regain my composure before we could say the last of our prayers together. There was a real long silence afterwards. It was Billy who broke the silence.

"You okay, Mr. Cameron?" he asked, opening his eyes again.

"No. No, I'm not." I paused, trying to sort out my thoughts. "This whole thing with you and Alex has me pretty shaken up."

"Why?"

"Well, I just wonder if I hadn't ..." I stopped. I had just backed myself into a very awkward verbal corner.

"If you hadn't beat up Alex, he wouldn't have tried to burn up my home? I nodded wordlessly.

"No. Doesn't work like that." Billy adjusted himself in the bed, sitting up a little higher to look me in the eyes. "You're not from these parts. You don't know Alex and you don't know our history. He's been beating me up ever since we were kids. The last time he did it, my Mom called the police chief and they told him that if he touched me again, they would toss him in jail. That would have wrecked his college career, so he's pretty much left me alone – at least physically." Billy leaned back against the pillow and sighed. "But I'm always good as the butt of his jokes."

"I'm sorry, Billy."

"You know, Mr. Cameron, Father Maurini tells us about forgiving those who are our enemies, but I haven't figured out how to do that yet." He looked down towards his feet and shook his head slowly from side to side. "I don't know how to tell you this, but there's a part of me that ..." He stopped, embarrassed, then plunged forward. "There's a part of me that thinks that Alex got just what he deserved. I'm really having hard time feeling sorry for him. That's what I told Fr. Maurini when he came to hear my confession last week. I was really mad at Alex and I still am."

Ouch. That hurt. And I told him so. I told him about my struggles with the same problem. The difference between us was that I learned how to defend myself. I told him how I put a stop to the bullying by putting a kid in the hospital.

"I almost killed him, Billy. Didn't mean to. I just forgot that there was a plate glass window behind me when I threw him. Cut him up real bad." I paused and looked away before continuing. "But you know the worst part is that I've never felt bad about what I did to him. Never. He was a big old nasty bully, and to this day I still can't help but feeling that I gave him the beating that he needed. Sorry? I don't feel it. I suppose I should, but I don't. Maybe that's something I need to confess next time I go to Mass."

We sat in silence for a while, then Billy spoke up again.

"You know what I'm going to do, Mr. Cameron? I'm going to go visit Alex tomorrow and I'm going to tell him I'm sorry that he got hurt. I don't really feel sorry, but I thought that perhaps if I went and saw him, I might somehow feel sorry for him. I understand he's been hurt pretty bad."

We talked for a few minutes more and then I left. I was pretty stunned by what Billy told me. If I had been Billy, I would have gone into Alex's room, pointed a finger at him and laughed myself silly – right in his face. Billy gave me an awful lot to think about that day.

Time passed and the boys healed and went their separate ways. I never found out what happened when Billy went in to see Alex. I don't think anyone else ever did either, or at least, if they did, no one talked about it.

It would make a lovely story to say that the incident caused Alex change his ways, but it didn't go down that way. Alex continued to be a mean jerk. He started drinking heavily a few months after he got out of the hospital. One night, played pool until three in the morning, got into a fight at the bar, and then drove off and wrapped his car around a tree at 110 miles an hour. It was gruesome, and the funeral was a closed casket service.

Billy lives in Minnesota now. I have a picture he sent me sitting on my desk at school. It's the same old Billy, but with some exceptional changes. His hair is cut short and parted at the side. He is standing next to his mother, wearing a nice shirt and well pressed khaki pants. He finally stopped chopping away at his beard and let it grow. Trimmed close to his face, I have to say that it gives him a nice overall look.

Every so often I get a letter from him. This was the most recent one he sent me:

"Dear Mr. Cameron,

I hope you are well and this letter finds you enjoying God's blessings. I was in the area last week and dropped by to see the old high school. I'm sorry I missed you. Guess I should have dropped you a note to let you know that I would be coming by. I hope you enjoyed your vacation.

Principal Pochino informed me that Alex Turner died in a car crash a while back. I was sorry to hear that. I really believe he had a hard time dealing with the scars from his burns and he never got over it. I am praying for the repose of his soul.

There's something I've wanted to tell you for a long time, but never found the right time to do so until now. I think with finding out about Alex's death, you need to know this. The day you came over to my table and talked to me saved my life. You see, I was just so tired of being lonely that I was going to go home that night and take a bottle of painkillers (my mother's prescription) and just put an end to it all. I had it all planned out. Your interest in my hobby made me change my mind. Since I was a kid I've been able to accept that I'm ugly to the bone. It took a while, but Mom helped me understand that physical good looks come one day and go the next, just like they did with Alex. It was not having any friends that I couldn't stand. I was just so lonely. You've been a good friend to me.

I just wanted you to know this because I know by our letters over the years that you sometimes blame yourself for Alex's burns, and I am hoping that you don't blame yourself for his death. Alex made his choice, and you didn't make him do what he did that night.

I've come to see that what God gives us in life is the cross we have to bear for our salvation. You made my cross bearable, and I will always be thankful to you for that.

Your friend, Billy.

It took me a while to stop crying after I put the letter down.

I think we look for grace in the wrong places. We look for the spectacular, but God's grace appears to us in the most unlikely places – an adult child who spends years quietly tending a sick and dying parent, a priest who goes back into the barrio after being shot and left for dead, an unwanted kid who will not let his worst enemy die when he would have every right to have done so.

TRUE HEARTS
OF THE
SAWTOOTH
RANGE

I remember the first time I saw him. The thing that struck me immediately were his eyes. They were a shade of blue I had never seen, and they almost seemed to leap out from his face to grab your attention. They were, without a doubt, the most beautiful eyes I had ever seen on man or beast, and this was a beast.

He was a wolf – the most magnificent wolf I had ever seen in my time in this country. I've seen a few since I moved out to Montana, but none have ever come close to him. From his nose to the tip of his tail, he was a regal being, a king of the forest in which he lived and moved about.

I guess I'm just a city dweller, a sap from the East, but I always tend to look at wolves as big, beautiful dogs. Of course, this is not true, and making the mistake of treating a wolf as if it is a dog can get a fella killed out here. My thinking is probably what caused me all my trouble.

After Annie died, I had a pretty rough time of it. It got to the point that all I could hear anymore was the noise in the city. Cars honking, motors roaring, machinery running– it was a constant barrage of noise, noise, noise until every day I just wanted to scream for it to stop. I remember the morning I was rudely awakened by a jerk outside my window playing his radio loud enough to share with the dead. I threw open the window and cursed him, his mother, and his whole rotten family. I guess I was lucky he was not much more than a kid or I would have probably had a fight on my hands. People in the city don't take kindly to that kind of response, so I lucked out. But that was the day I realized I either had to leave New York or something bad was going to happen.

Montana is...well, gosh, how do I describe it? It was pretty much what I imagined, and exactly what I needed at that point in my life.

I drove west until the mountains greeted me outside a little town called Choteau. After a bit of negotiation, I bought a small cabin near the foot of the Sawtooth Mountain Range, half an hour north of town. I wasn't here two weeks before I realized that the quiet and solitude was helping me a lot in dealing with Annie's death. How does a young woman who never smoked a day in her life die from lung cancer? I needed time to be alone with a reality I didn't want to face. I'm not proud of this, but there were nights I would go out into the fields outside my cabin, look up at more stars than I ever imagined existing, and scream at God for letting it happen. I haven't lost my faith, but let's just say that I'm still struggling to trust Him after all that has happened.

Of course, meeting Sam Clybourne didn't help that much either. Sam is one of the locals. He was born on a sheep ranch and he will die a sheep rancher

– if I don't kill him first. Everyone in town knows him and most folks know to leave him alone. Sam is his own man. He does what he wants to do and he doesn't really care if you like it or not. I'll put it bluntly– even his Baptist religion doesn't make him a nice fella to know. It would have been good for me if I could have just stayed out of his road, but that wasn't to be, which makes me wonder why God allowed that to happen also.

My first run-in with Sam came about because of the wolf. Sheep and cattle ranching are big here in Montana. Unfortunately, they don't coexist well with the wolves, who regard the ranches as a kind of rolling buffet, especially if deer and elk herds have not been productive for them. We've got a couple of lawsuits going on out here between the ranchers and the animal lovers. The ranchers managed to convince the U.S. government to let them shoot wolves and coyotes from the air, which infuriated the animal lovers. They, in turn, filed a couple of lawsuits and got an injunction against the flyover shootings. That led to a whole mess of bad feelings in town and a couple of arrests, Sam being one of them. He happened to bump into one of the animal lovers one morning over breakfast. Words ensued and Sam left a couple of the guy's teeth on the floor, which got him arrested for assault. It also set a tone for what happened with me and the wolf.

I like to drive up to the foot of the mountains and walk in the woods. Gives me time to think. Sometimes I try to pray, but I mostly just walk around and think.

The wolf was lying against a tree, at first, I thought he was sleeping. Scared me silly. He was a huge wolf and I was afraid for my life when I first saw him. I was trying to back away quietly when I stepped on a stick or something. At the sound, the wolf opened his eyes, bared his fangs, and growled at me, but he didn't move. It took me a few seconds to realize that something was wrong with him. I stopped backing up and tried to get a closer look at him. He tried to stand up, still growling at me, but his rear legs wouldn't leave the ground.

I wasn't about to risk getting close to him. I went back to the cabin, got in my Jeep and drove into town. I knew a veterinarian, Doc Jones, who was sympathetic to the plight of the wolves and brought him out to the woods with me to see the wolf. He used a dart gun to tranquilize the wolf so we could get a closer look at what was wrong.

Someone had shot the poor beast. Doc found out later the bullet went right through his spine and paralyzed his rear legs. We went to Doc's van, got a litter out to carry the wolf, and took him into town to see if we could save his life.

Of course, Sam had to be passing by at the moment we were unloading the wolf from Doc Jones' van. Why does life have to be that way?

"What the hell you got there?" Sam was being his normal unfriendly self, but now his voice had a threatening tone to it. "If that's a damn wolf, you better be taking him in there to put him to sleep." He stood on the sidewalk, his lips pursed in anger, his fists balled at his sides. He looked all the world for a man who wanted to rush us and kill the wolf with his own two hands.

"Sam, go mind your own damn business," Doc Jones responded in an equally unfriendly voice.

"You better not be healing that wolf," Sam yelled at us as we disappeared into the clinic. He said something else after the door was shut, but I didn't make out what it was. Doc came around me and turned the lock on the door, muttering something under his breath. I didn't get it all, but I did hear the word "idiot" among others. No love lost between these two men.

Doc called me up three days later.

"Your wolf is going to live," he announced factually. "Now comes the problem of what to do with him." I told him I'd be down shortly to see the wolf; to which he informed me that I shouldn't exactly expect a happy homecoming from the wolf. "He's pretty well mad at the world, and I can't say I blame him all that much."

Yeah, the wolf was not a happy camper. I would think getting shot would do that to just about anybody, but especially to an animal who was going about his business and had no way of understanding why he couldn't walk anymore. Wolves are pretty smart animals and he probably figured out some man had done this to him. He was none too happy to see either one of us and gave us an impressive display of his fangs to express that displeasure. I tried to talk to him and he gave me a deep, angry growl.

"Oh, great!" I said, sighing and leaning back against a table. "Now what?" I turned to look at Doc Jones. "Is there any way to tame him? I hate to think of putting him down."

"It's been done, but it's gonna take a lot of work on your part. And you aren't gonna make a whole pile of friends around here keeping a wolf."

So what? Like I really cared. Doc was right though. It did take a lot of work. And a lot of pain. Doc tranquilized him for the ride back to the cabin and he gave me clear instructions about what I was to do, but I didn't listen all that well. I got bitten three times for a total of 128 stitches. The last time the wolf got me, he tore up the tendon in my right hand. I was trying to feed him from my hand. He took the meat I was offering and then, before I knew it, he turned like lightening and nailed me right across my open hand. Like I said, I kept thinking of him as a big dog instead of a wild animal, which was pretty stupid. My pinky finger to this day doesn't work right. The last time I showed up at Teton Medical Center to get stitched up, the doctor on duty all but called me a fool.

The howling started the second night I had him with me. He was lying on the floor by the fireplace where I kept him and suddenly his ears perked up. Another wolf was howling outside the cabin, and it was real close, which surprised me. Most of the howling I heard at night took place further up in the mountains, not this close. Wolves don't like the smell of man and they didn't usually get close to my cabin.

His response howl was awesome – and deafening. It didn't take me long to figure out what was happening.

"Lord have mercy! Is that your mate calling for you?" I spoke the question out loud and he turned to look at me. Well now what do I do? I was still thinking about it when they started up again. I think the only way I can describe it is two broken-hearted lovers crying out for each other. It went on most of the night and I got precious little sleep.

I called Doc Jones the next day and told him about it. He came up after the clinic closed, shot a tranquilizer into the wolf, and we took him outside and laid him on a blanket with a pile of raw meat nearby. He came around just as the first star of the night peeked over the distant Rocky Mountain range. When he cleared his head, he sniffed the meat, then gave a loud howl, which was immediately answered.

We didn't have to wait long. Another wolf appeared at the edge of the woods. She stopped and sniffed the air warily, then slowly approached the cabin. When she saw her mate, she broke into a full gallop and threw herself on him.

"She's pregnant."

"You can tell that from here?"

"I'm a vet, remember?" Doc kinda laughed when he said it, then went on. "Yeah, and I'd say she's due about any day now, judging from her size."

We watched their joyful reunion. I was a little choked up watching it because I couldn't help but think of Annie. As she leaped around him and nuzzled him, I found myself wondering if that's what heaven is like when we get there and see our loved ones. *Damn, I miss Annie!*

"You got an extra bed in this joint?" Doc's question interrupted my thoughts.

"You planning on staying the night?"

"Yeah, and if you're smart, you won't go out of this cabin either until she is long gone, which will probably be tomorrow morning." He watched her lay down next to her mate and grab a piece of meat to chew on. "If either one of us goes out of this cabin tonight, she'll tear our throats out to protect him. So I'm not leaving."

It was a long night. Doc's been player poker a lot longer than I have and he cleaned me out for about $200 bucks. But between the good company and watching our wolves, I don't think I'd spent a better night since I got here.

❀❀❀❀❀

I started calling him Jake. I can't tell you why. For some reason, the name came to me, so Jake it was. I know it sounds sappy, but I named his mate Annie.

Yeah, as in my sweet wife, who would have loved being with me and seeing them together. Annie loved all kinds of animals, and I think she would have really loved this place and all the creatures that live and fly around my cabin. I sit on my front porch and watch bald eagles fly overhead and wonder why I didn't come out here years ago.

Doc was right about Annie. She came around for a few more nights, then she disappeared for a week. At first I was afraid that some bounty hunter had shot her, but Doc told me that she probably had birthed her pups and wouldn't leave them for a while. I kept on feeding Jake and left chunks of meat at the edge of the woods. Doc told me that eventually Annie would have to come out of her den and find something to eat and I would be doing her a favor to put out meat.

I was watching TV one night about two weeks later when I heard an unusual commotion outside. When I went to the window to look, there was

Annie with six roly-poly little pups dancing around her and playing with their daddy. They made a heck of a racket until about one o'clock, then she rounded them up and they disappeared back into the woods. I found out later that she had taken quite a risk bringing them out because bear and even large owls will prey upon a small pup.

I saw a National Geographic program one night about rehabilitation of paralyzed animals. There was a dog on the program, paralyzed just like Jake. The owner had a contraption made that looked like a miniature racing sulky and put the dog's hindquarters into it. The program showed the dog trotting around the house, going through the park, and for all intents and purposes, acting just as if its legs were working.

I made a bunch of phone calls and finally managed to get the producer of the show. He listened to my situation sympathetically, then gave me the phone number for the company that had fabricated the rig. I asked Doc to give them the specs on Jake and they sent me a finished product a month later.

When I got the carriage, I had Doc come out and put Jake to sleep. We put his hindquarters in the canvas pouch with his legs dangling from either side. Then we opened a couple of beers and waited for him to wake up.

It took Jake a couple of minutes to realize that he could move around using his front legs. When he got the hang of it, he started trotting all over the yard until he wore himself out and collapsed in a heap, his front lying on the ground and his rear end hanging in the air in the canvas pouch. It was comical. Hilarious really. I started to laugh at him. He opened one eye and regarded me with what I can only describe as a look of pure disgust.

"I don't think he likes you laughing at him," Doc chortled, barely stifling a laugh himself.

Jake slowly stood up and looked at the both of us, and then something miraculous happened. He walked slowly towards the porch where we were sitting, his eyes fixed on us.

"Don't move." Doc ordered. "Just hold real still and see if he does what I think he is going to do."

Jake walked up to the edge of the porch, lowered his head a little, and rubbed the side of his head against my pants leg. I have to admit that I was scared, but I was thrilled, too. Finally, I couldn't help myself and slowly extended my hand towards his head, stopping it just inches away from that mouthful of sharp teeth that had given me such pain in the past. Jake turned his head up to me and licked my hand. Then without a sound, he backed up a few inches, turned in his cart, and went to lie down on his blanket.

"That is the craziest thing I've ever seen," Doc mused, his voice filled with amazement. "I think you've made a friend for life."

I only wish it could have been so.

It took a while for Annie to warm up to me. After all, like Jake, she was a wild animal with a natural and instinctive fear of man. Despite all the hype about wolves, they are timid creatures when it comes to interacting with man, and they have plenty of reason to be. Ranchers out here do their level best to kill them on sight. It's a bad intersection between wolf and man that has caused all this misery for them. They don't know that the sheep being kept at these ranches aren't meant as food for them. They just do what comes naturally and the ranchers, in turn, do what comes naturally to men who see their profits being dragged away and eaten at night.

I fed Annie for weeks before she finally came up to me one evening and introduced herself to me. Jake actually brought her to me. I guess he told her in wolf talk *"Look, this fella's not like the rest of those human beings."* And she was willing to give me a chance. It was a lot scarier having her approach me than it was with my first meeting with Jake. Remember, Jake was paralyzed and couldn't move. Annie was lithe and fast and I could imagine her going for my throat in a heartbeat. But she never turned on me. Jake led her up to me and I held real still and let her sniff me until she was content that I was no threat and turned away to tend to her pups. She did this for several nights, then one night she put her muzzle into my hand and licked my palm. The next night I put a steak in my hand and let her take it from me.

Over the summer I managed to make friends with her and her pups. I had a glorious summer with them, but I was always very slow when I moved and very cautious around Annie and the pups.

I was in town one Saturday, getting some supplies at Melton's Mercantile for the coming winter, when Sam Clybourne walked into the store. I was all set to ignore him, but I guess men like Sam just have to start trouble when they are in a bad mood. I was heading for the door when he yelled at me.

"Hey, city boy! Whatever happened to that stinkin' wolf you brought into town?'

I didn't answer him and pushed on through the door. The next thing I knew, I heard the door slam open behind me and felt a large, rough hand on my shoulder. Sam spun me around and glared down at me.

"I'm talkin' to you, hoss!" He gave me a little shove to let me know that he meant business. "What'd you do with that mangy critter? And don't lie to me, you hear?"

I wish I had learned to defend myself when I was a kid. My Momma used to keep me from fighting, which put me at a real disadvantage. It would have been nice to have been able to pound the Sam into the ground, but it would have never happened, as I found out later. I guess Sam grew up chewin' nails as a kid. You know, *that* kind of tough. I gave a swallow and then decided to just tell him the truth and be done with it.

"He's out at my cabin. Look here, Mr. Clybourne, he isn't gonna bother you or your sheep. He's paralyzed and he can't get around." I felt Sam's hand tighten on my shoulder in anger. "I'm telling you, he's just a big dog to me. I feed him and take care of him and he won't bother your sheep. I promise."

"We'll see about that," he growled. I don't think I've ever seen a man with as mean a look in his eyes as I saw that day. I thought he was going to slug me right then, but instead he suddenly shoved me away, spilling my groceries all over the ground, and turned away cursing under his breath.

I don't know how Sam knew that I wasn't at my cabin. Maybe one of his cronies saw me drive through town on the way to Helena and ran off to tell him. Doesn't matter. All I know is that when I came back, I found Jake lying dead in a pool of blood. His beautiful blue eyes were still open, staring lifelessly at the sky.

I don't remember how long I held him and cried, but I knew instantly who had done this, and when I was done burying him, I got in my car and headed into town. I had a pretty good idea where I would find the culprit.

Sam was right where I expected to find him.

I strode fast across the floor of the saloon, almost running. I stopped a foot from him, my fists clenched and my heart filled with a rage I had never felt in all my life. "You killed Jake!" I screamed. He looked down at me and started laughing. "So what?" he spat out, eyeing me with contempt.

I don't think Sam expected me, or anybody for that matter, to ever take a swing at him. He's got a reputation in town as the meanest son-of-a-bitch that ever walked on two feet, a man who has put more than one man in the hospital, but at that moment I didn't care. My punch caught him by surprise. I hit him square on the nose and drove him back into the wall. He slammed against the wall, his knees buckled a bit, then he stood up, wiped away the blood trickling over his lips, and gave me a nasty looking grin that made my blood run cold.

"Sonny boy, I'm gonna enjoy this."

He probably did. I tried to fight him, but he beat me up real good. I think he might have killed me except that a couple of his buddies managed to pull him off me, telling him I wasn't worth going to prison. Paul, the bartender, called 911 and they took me over to the medical center, but after the folks there got a good look at me, they called the air ambulance from Helena to come get me. I was bruised up good, had two broken ribs, and looked like a raccoon with my two black eyes. I spent a two nights in St. Peter's Hospital to be sure I didn't have any internal bleeding. Then, to add insult to injury, I had to spend money on a bus ticket to get back to Choteau.

A couple of nights after I came back home I evened the score. I put on a heavy coat on and Sam never saw the pistol I pulled out from my belt. I guess he didn't expect the city boy to have a gun, but I had bought one for protection when I went to walk in the woods. It was an older model Colt .45 I got from a cowboy who needed the money and was willing to part with it at a good price.

I came into the bar where he was having a drink and walked right up to him with my hat in my hands, trying to look real humble. He kind of grinned and started to get up and that was when I dropped to my knees.

"Mr. Clybourne, I'm sorry. I came in to apologize to you and ask you to please not hurt me anymore."

He started laughing real loud and called me a few names. I was still kneeling in front of him when I put the pistol flat against his left kneecap and pulled the trigger. The blast made my ears ring and I didn't hear him scream in pain. He dropped to the floor and started rolling around. I grabbed his right ankle, put the barrel of the gun against his right knee and pulled the trigger again. A second later one of Sam's buddies nailed me to the floor with a flying tackle and grabbed my gun hand.

I was told later that the only reason I'm alive today is that one of the town's police officers just happened to be in the bar having a drink when this all went down. From the story I got, there were at least six pistols pulled on me, then the cop fired a shot in the air and everyone froze. That probably saved my life. I'm sure Sam's buddies would have happily filled me with lead and then claimed self-defense in court.

Assault with a weapon, a felony in Montana, is punishable by a term in the state prison of up to twenty years and a fine of up to $50,000. After he heard the whole story from me, Judge Williamson sentenced me to one to three years. I got the feeling that he didn't much care for Sam. I watched his eyes while during the trial and they got dark when Sam was testifying.

"Well, Sam," I heard him intone as I was being led out of the courtroom. "You finally pissed off someone with balls enough to stand up to you." I think the light sentence was his way of letting Sam know that he was pretty well fed up with Sam and his whole approach to life.

I stayed to myself in the prison. I wasn't interested in making "buddies" in there. I just wanted to get out and get back home, and the sooner the better

A priest came in once a week from Butte. When he found out I'm Catholic, he stopped by my cell to visit. He listened to my story without making me feel like I was wasting his time. He moved his mouth kind of funny and then told me I needed to think more on what Jesus did to the men who crucified Him.

"I can't hear your confession, Larry, unless you are really repentant, and it sounds like you need to work on that a bit." Father Barkett handed me a small New Testament. "Read the 23rd chapter of Luke's Gospel every night this week and think about what Jesus did to the men who crucified Him."

I tried. Honest I did. I read and re-read that passage, but every time I went to Confession, I had to be truthful and admit that while I knew what I did was wrong, I didn't feel bad about it and I wasn't feeling particularly forgiving.

Maybe sometime in the future God will help me see things differently, but for right now, I still think Sam got what was coming to him.

I minded my own business and buttered up every man uniform I could see while I made sure to obey every rule in the prison. For this, I managed to get an early parole. I hope the parole office doesn't find out, but when I returned home, I stopped in the saloon where Sam likes to hangout. The minute I came through the door, everyone stopped talking. I walked right up to him and looked him dead in the eyes.

"I'm out of prison now," I growled at him. "You keep to yourself and I'll leave you alone and we'll be fine, but if I catch you anywhere near my place, I'll shoot you on sight." I took a step back and let him stew on that for a minute.

"You think I'm a city boy? I got news for you. I grew up in Pennsylvania. We hunt deer every year and I've shot my share. I know guns, and I don't have any problem hitting a buck from 100 yards." I paused for effect. "And I won't have any trouble hitting *you* either."

Then I turned and strode out of the saloon. But before I did, I got a funny look from him as he slowly nodded his head back at me, a look I had never seen in his eyes in the short time I'd known him. It was a combination of respect and maybe a little bit of fear. Someone had finally been crazy enough to stand up to him and give him a taste of his own bitter medicine.

I put the cabin up for sale, but a month later I called the agent and had her come get the sign. It occurred to me one day that if I were to cut and run Sam would win, and I wasn't about to let that happen.

I don't go into town anymore. I found a kid who likes to be paid for picking up my groceries and running errands. I just want to be alone now. At night I come out to the porch about eight o'clock and watch the sun disappear behind the mountains until the first star appears and purple and blue hues cast themselves over the sky, dimming, dimming, dimming into a great black blanket filled with glittering pinpoints of light. You have never really seen stars until you look at them on a moonless Montana night.

When the sun goes down, the singing begins. The song rolls down across the mountains and through the woods, first one voice and then dozens of others to join the song, the wolves taking up their chorus for the evening. I imagine I can hear Annie calling out among them. There many voices, and somewhere in there she is with them, calling out for one who is no longer with her.

Sitting on my porch, I close my eyes and immerse my senses in the cool Fall air. I take a deep breath and smell the rich smells of the forest, and I raise my head and I join their chorus.

I hope Annie hears my song.

SACRAMENT

Isabella Martin sat in her wheelchair, staring intently at the stranger in the hospital bed. A woman, a stranger unknown, who had shot her husband and left him for dead before turning the gun on herself. Despite five bullets fired at close range at her husband before placing the gun to her temple and pulling the trigger, both of them were alive.

"Revenge, Father. That's what it had to be. She was getting even with John before she died."

"Poor woman. What a terrible price she is paying for something that happened between John and her so very long ago."

The priest turned to look out the window, lost in his thoughts about John and this woman whom he had only heard of in a terrible confession made to him a long time ago in the privacy of Confession before the icon of Christ in his Byzantine Catholic parish. He had watched John grow spiritually from the day of that confession to the day he met Isabella, married her, and brought her into the parish as his wife. And now this.

"Sin pays a terrible wage when we employ it."

"She's a sad story from John's past," Isabella began, "She..."

"I know the story, Isabella," the priest replied, holding up his hand to stop her. "The whole story. John shared it with me in Confession years ago. And since he shared it with me in the Sacrament, I can't speak of it with you. I know – and that is all I am going to say or allow to be said of it because of the Seal of Confession."

"Okay, Father. As a Catholic I certainly respect that." She sat in the wheelchair, quietly rubbing her hands together in gentle circles as her mind wandered over the chaos of the events that had so suddenly turned her world upside down. Finally she spoke up.

"John must have given her AIDS and she came back to get revenge."

"Isabella, please. I know this is difficult, but I really don't wish to talk about any parts of this." He walked over to where the wheelchair sat, dragging a small chair behind him. He sat directly in front of Isabella and looked straight into her eyes.

"Look, I'm under constraint of my vows. Even if we are not talking directly about the incident, this is still part of it to me. But I think you're wrong. In order for John to have done that, he would have to be infected himself, and he isn't. Now, please. Let's let this work itself out without further talk about it." He wrapped his arms around Isabella and drew her close to him. "I am here for you. And God is still in charge, despite how all this looks."

Isabella nodded numbly. She hadn't put that piece of the puzzle in there. Of course. If John did have AIDS, then this would make sense – but he didn't.

Why then did she come back to do what she had done? Revenge for the rape that had taken place so long ago? What would have made her wait almost thirty years to find John and try to kill him?

"Okay, Father. Let's not talk about the incident. But what about her? What would make her wait almost thirty years to come back and seek revenge?"

"Dying." It was said in a matter of fact way. The old priest disengaged from her and looked into her eyes. "Dying does strange things to people. Old wounds are brought up that have to be dealt with. Sometimes people seek revenge, sometimes the wounds are talked about between people and forgiven. And sometimes I have seen people struggle with the hurts they have and yet in the end do nothing about them."

Isabella turn her wheelchair to the window and stared off into space, watching cars go by on the road below them. How would she handle this? Would she be able to help John? Would he let her? For the first two years after her accident she had been unwilling to hear anyone's advice, and with nasty retorts, refused their prayers when they came to visit. She had driven off a number of aides sent to care for her. It had taken two very special events to turn her life around. She let her mind wander back to a cold day in December when the first one took place.

❁❁❁❁❁

"There's a visitor at your door, Miss Isabella."

"I know. I can hear, Charlie."

"You want me to let him in?"

"Who is he?"

"I dunno. He says he needs to see you."

"What the hell. Let him in and see what his story is."

There was nothing special to the eye about the man who came through her front door and stood staring at Isabella. Her first thought was that he was a homeless person looking for a handout Then she observed that he was neatly dressed and well-groomed, unlike some of the panhandlers who frequented the street corners of her town. The only oddity about him was his empty left sleeve, neatly pinned to the side of his shirt. He looked uncomfortable, a man who appeared to want to speak but was having trouble finding the words as he approached the kitchen where Isabella sat in her wheelchair.

"Isabella Martin?"

"Yeah. That's me. What's your story?"

He started to speak, a few stuttering words flowing from his tightly pursed lips, then more silence, and all he could do was to stare at her until she curtly told him to either spit it out or get out. With that, a tear formed at the corner of each eye, rolling down his cheeks, following by others as he begin to sob.

"I'm so sorry," he managed to gasp as he sunk to his knees to the floor. His crying began in earnest, sobbing and saying "I'm sorry" over and over between gasps of breath. It took Isabella about a minute to put the whole picture together in her mind. When she did, she was not in a forgiving mood.

"You're the rotten bastard who did this to me!" she exclaimed in a loud, angry voice. She paused, feeling all the fury of her anger at having been put in a wheelchair, of having lost her marriage and her house - everything - to this man groveling and weeping before her. *"How dare you come to my house!"*

Before her aide, Charlie, could react, she had grabbed the entire plate of food sitting in front of her and flung it all over the unwelcome visitor. The plate missed him by inches, and she would have been glad at that moment if it had smacked him square in the face.

Charlie leaped between them, shielding him from any further flying objects. Turning to the man now lying on the floor, Charlie picked him up and began to gently but firmly push the visitor towards the front door. After a few steps, the man resisted.

"You need to go, sir. You done said your piece."

"No, I haven't," the visitor replied, a sudden determination to his voice. *"I practiced what I was going to say all the way over here."* His voice stiffened. *"I need to finish. I have to say this. Let me finish, please."* His voice was firm but pleading, and for some reason, Charlie relented.

"Okay. But you finish whatever you want to say and then you be on your way, you hear? No monkey business. Now say it and get out"

When the man turned to her and began to speak, Isabella once again ordered him out of her house, mixing her commands with a volume of angry Italian swear words. There was no way she was listening to anything that he had to say. He simply lowered his head and let it all come to him. All the anger, the fury and rage that had been bottled up inside her for so long now had a target - the man whose stupidity had put her in this wheelchair many years ago. She swore, she spit at him several times, her hands stretched out in a vain desire to reach him and perform their desired vengeance on him. Charlie tried to stop her, but his gentle, soft voice was no match for her Italian temper and operatic voice.

Finally, one last *"bastardo!"* flew from her lips before she stopped, slumped over, exhausted and sobbing softly, her anger temporarily abated.

"You don't know how sorry I am that I did this to you and your friends. His voice filled the silence with a new sound - a man in deep regret, trying to make right something that could never be right. *"When I found out that I had killed people with my boat, it almost drove me crazy. We were just having a party and a good time. I turned around a second to talk with my friends and then suddenly, there was your boat."* He stopped to take a deep breath before continuing. Isabella had lifted her head and was looking at him intently.

"I just got out of prison a couple of months ago."

"You deserve it. You should rot in there. I hope you rot in hell."

"I know. I had nightmares in prison about what I did. I would wake up screaming at night. They took me to the prison psychiatrist and that didn't help. When I got out, I figured I ought to go to church and maybe finding God would help me. After I got saved, the pastor told me that the only way I would ever get any peace about it would if you forgave me for what I did.

I know you hate me now and I don't blame you one bit. But I'm going to ask you to forgive me. If you ever can, all I ask is that you call me and just forgive me. I'm so sorry that I did this to you."

He put a piece of paper in Charlie's hand and then turned and walked out the door without another word. It would be almost a full year later when Charlie retrieved the paper from where he placed it.

❖❖❖❖❖

"What are you thinking of?" Father Theo's gentle voice broke in on her memories of that meeting.

"Thinking back..." a pause to bring herself back to the reality of now... to when I was paralyzed."

"I kind of thought so. What in particular?"

Isabella remained quiet, embarrassed to admit to what they both knew. She had been a witch on wheels to be around. The stranger's visit did not mitigate things - only made them worse. Everyone but God caught the anger, and only because Isabella feared hell did she not give Him a piece of her mind. Nonetheless, some nights her prayers were angry and demanding. Her once-strong Catholic faith was shattered and unable to turn away her pain. She knew what the Church taught, had heard the lessons on forgiving and accepted them, but when she found herself in the middle of the reality of needing to forgive someone who had terrible sinned against her, she found it impossible.

"Just remembering how hard it was for me to forgive Tom Snellinger for the accident." She looked at Father with an awkward smile, then lowered her eyes in embarrassment. "I was not exactly pleasant to be around."

"That's what I heard. I imagine you had go through a lot to come to the place where you were really able to forgive him."

"I did, Father," she agreed. "The worst part of it all is that I'm a cradle Catholic. I was taught to forgive people as a little girl sitting in my mother's lap. I wonder just how hard it's going to be for John as a convert to the faith."

"That, my dear, is the sixty-four thousand dollar question. I have a feeling that he is going to need not only a great deal of our prayers, but as much patience as you have to give and then some. I'm willing to bet that unless God does something miraculous for him while he's in his coma, he's going to have a period of real anger with Sara, especially when he finds out he's paralyzed." Father paused. "I'm also concerned that he may be quite angry with God. Wouldn't be the first time someone has been mad with God when tragedy hits. The good news is that God's love can overcome even that."

"I know, Father." Isabella leaned forward in her wheelchair to stroke her husband's hand. "Do I ever know."

❀❀❀❀❀

The mysterious ways of God. His plans and purposes for us. Who can really know them? You think that life is headed one way and you find yourself walking an entirely different path. Then, just when you least expect it, He shows up and says, "Let's have an adventure!"

Isabella chucked, remembering the day she found the phrase in a booklet of devotional literature. *"Let's have an adventure."* it said of God's desire to draw us into His plans. The book had been cheerily speaking of God as the One Who comes to us and draws us out of our shells of self-pity and invites us to come on an adventure called life. She had been reading it at Charlie's insistence, his hope that perhaps something could reach into her bitter heart and begin the healing of her wounds.

With a particularly nasty oath, she threw the book across the room.

"Have an adventure my..."

"Miss Isabella!" Charlie admonished her softly before the next word came out. He sighed, shaking his head softly, and picked up the book.

"Okay, what got you all riled up this morning?" he asked as he placed it back in front of her.

Dear, kind Charlie. So unflappable for month after month since coming to be her aide. He quietly put up with her nasty comments. If she was too nasty, he would simply go do some chore around the house and then show up an hour later when she had calmed down. Always he tried to bring her out of her depression and anger over being wheelchair bound.

"This!" she snarled, pointing to the still open page, held open for her by a paper clip. Her finger zoomed in on the offending phrase. Charlie read quietly without comment, then pulled up a nearby chair, leaned back, and gave her a smile.

"Well, I think that's just a lovely idea. No one said the adventure had to be fun. Yours is challenging. What is God challenging you to do? What is He challenging you to become?"

"Easy for you to say," she snorted. *"You're not sitting here paralyzed.*

Look here, Miss Isabella. Number one, you're not dead. Therefore, number two, there's a reason for this, as hard as that may seem to you. You haven't even tried to find the reason for it. Why are you still here, Miss Isabella?

God isn't trying to punish you. There's something for you to learn in all this. But you aren't listening. You are so caught up in your misery and enjoying your anger that you don't want to stop and try to figure this thing out. And all the while, you just keep getting more and more unhappy."

Charlie settled back in his chair, the smile slowly replaced with a look Isabella had never seen before. *"I never much speak about this, Miss Isabella. It's kind private. My son was eighteen when the Klansmen found him walking home on the road from Tahalla."* He shifted in the chair and cleared his throat before he continued. His voice began low, with a tone Isabella had never heard before.

"Someone had raped a white woman. Someone black. Those boys were looking for anyone they could find and they found my son." He paused again, trying to adjust to the pain of a history long since set aside and deliberately forgotten.

"They wasn't much left of him when they found him. It took the coroner three days to identify my boy. Then they told me about it, but they wouldn't let me see his body. They said he was so messed up the shock might kill me." He paused – a deep sigh – then continued. *"I never even got to say a proper goodbye to him."*

"I knew who done it. I think everyone in Tahalla knew because we all knew who was in the Klan. But couldn't nothing be done. One of the boys was the mayor's son.

I stewed on that for a couple of months. Got good and angry, just like you. I even thought about gettin' my old hunting rifle and taking the law in my own hands." A single tear formed at the corner of Charlie's eye. It poised for a second, then began to wend its way down his cheek. *"He was my baby. The only child we ever had."*

"I was sittin' in church one day. Can't exactly remember what the preacher said, but when he was done, I knew what I had to do. I went over to the

mayor's house and knocked on the door that same Sunday afternoon. I guess it musta been God helping me, because the mayor's boy answered the door.

I stood there and looked at him for a long time. He was a nice-looking boy. Shame he had such a black heart. He finally says to me 'What you want, nigger?'

I just told him 'I want you to know that I forgive you for what you done to my son.' Didn't stick around for no talk neither. Just turned and walked away. But you know something, Miss Isabella? When I did, I was a free man."

Charlie drew out the word 'free' and let his smile return. "Yes, ma'am. *I was truly free. My son loved Jesus and I was sure he was in heaven. I was not going to be in the hell of hatred for the rest of my life over what this white boy did.*

You need to do the same, Miss Isabella. You gonna suffer the rest of your life if you don't, and God isn't going to come git you either. He will let you stay here and suffer until you learn how to forgive this man."

How is it that we can read the same passage in a book, hear the same advice given to us as before, and suddenly it's as if we really hear it for the first time? He had told this to her a couple of times before in various ways, but each time she had blown him off. That morning his story and his words sunk into her heart. He was right. She was reveling in her sorrow, enjoying being the most miserable person she could be to everyone. She would get even with the whole world, one person at a time, no matter how long it took. Now an inner eye was open, a light of truth showing her as she really was – a nasty, miserable shew making life wretched for herself and everyone around her.

She began to cry.

Charlie gently reached to give her a hug, letting her hold onto him until tears couldn't come any longer, giving way to silence and soft, occasional sobs.

"What do I do, Charlie? I'm so angry inside."

"What's done is done. There ain't no turning back to git your old life back. You have to accept that this is life now and you have people who care for you. You have to turn to them now. And to Jesus."

"No one cares. No one comes to visit me."

"Well, Miss Isabella," Charlie cleared his throat before continuing. *"you kinda scared them all off, you know?"*

She opened her mouth to reply, but no sound came out. Then there was a kind of stifled laugh, followed by a snort as she faced the irony of her self-pitying statement. She had even driven away her closest friends from high school. Only her mother came down from New York to see her occasionally, and Isabella realized that she had shortened her mother's visits with her constant griping and bitter spirit.

Charlie took her shaking hands in his. *"I care about you Miss Isabella. Someday I hope I can see you happy again."*

She smiled at the aged black man on one knee in front of her. How had she been so fortunate to get such a kind gentleman from the aide agency? He was a part-timer. Retired from the railroad. Member of the local Baptist church. He worked about 20 hours a week as an aide and he was a good one.

"That's all Miss Susan will let me work," he told her when they had first met, referring to his wife of 50 years.

Miss Susan. It was a habit from the Old South where Charlie was born and raised. In Mississippi, young and old, every woman was "Miss." Miss Susan, his wife. Miss Louise, the agency manager. Miss Abbey, the girl who replaced Charlie every night. Miss Isabella. When she was not in a foul mood, she found the habit quite charming. And Charlie was always charming. Even when she was short-tempered with him, he somehow never took it personally. When her tirades were over, and she would somehow find it in her to apologize to him, he would say *"That's okay, Miss Isabella. Jesus loves you."*

"Well, if Jesus loves me so much, how about you pray that He takes me outta here?" That was always her bitter retort whenever he said that to her. She was having none of a love that would let a drunken sailor in a speedboat kill her friends and ruin her life. She plainly wanted to die, and made no secret of informing Charlie of that, as well as telling God in her prayers that she wanted Him to take her out of this world. A couple of times she had made that request known to God with some pretty coarse language.

And now she sat in her wheelchair, for the first time in years with a different feeling in her heart. The harsh reality of her meanness to the world, her unforgiving spirit, and even the way she had been so mean to Charlie.

"I'm so sorry, Charlie. I've been so mean to you and all you've ever tried to do is to help me."

"I forgive you, Miss Isabella." Charlie's face softened into a gentle smile. *"I been forgiving you for a long time now. I knew you was hurtin'"* He took her hand between his and gently rubbed it. *"And I been praying for you for a long time, too."*

"What do I do now, Charlie?" She raised her eyes to the sky. *"Lord, what a fool I've been!"*

"What did your Momma teach you? I know she raised you right. I can see it all over your walls."

He was referring to the pictures of Christ and the Virgin Mary scattered around the house. Even in her anger, Isabella had let them stay up for some reason. And occasionally, when she was in a half decent mood, she would turn to the familiar prayers of the Rosary, trying in vain to find some comfort against the anger consuming her life.

Charlie rose quietly and left, heading down the hallway of her house. When he returned, he was holding her Rosary in his hand, the beads spilling out between his fingers. He smiled at the large and colorful beads, rolled them around in his hand a little bit, then handed them to her.

"I don't know much about this Rosary thing you do, but you know, you Catholics sure have a pretty religion. Even your church is pretty." His hand reached out. *"Here. I'll leave you alone while I do some laundry."* With a nod and a smile, he disappeared wordlessly down the hall.

No great change can take place overnight. It was simply the morning she began her own adventure, an adventure into a world of forgiveness she had only heard about before.

Little by little Isabella made a deliberate efforts to look for anything to enjoy in each day. When spring came, she had Charlie roll her wheelchair outside so she could smell the ocean and listen to the birds sing. She tuned her TV to EWTN and began to listen to Mother Angelica and other programs to help her repair her broken faith. Her pastor was surprised when she showed up for Mass one Sunday morning and asked him to hear her confession. After a long recitation sins she had committed against people, her heart felt strangely different. The bitterness was gone, replaced with a peace which she had never experienced before.

When Lent began that year, she went to Mass to receive ashes. A visiting priest, an old friend her pastor had known at seminary, gave the sermon she needed to hear. It was about not just thinking of forgiveness, but the practical ways of making forgiveness real, including the importance of telling people that they were forgiven. The visiting priest spoke a long time on the necessity of forgiveness in the Christian life and how forgiveness could heal both the forgiven one and the forgiver. When she got arrived home, she knew what she needed to do.

"Charlie, do you remember the man who hit me with the speedboat? The man who came here months ago?"

Charlie never said a word. He went over to the kitchen cabinet and took out a tin box. Inside was a small yellow slip of paper. Charlie picked up the phone and began to dial the number on the paper.

"You know, Miss Isabella, I really like your religion. If I wasn't such a Baptist, I might think of joining your church."

He gave a gentle laugh at the idea, then put the phone to her ear so she could talk. She looked up at him as the phone began to ring. He could see the confusion in her eyes.

"You'll be just fine, Miss Isabella. You just do what you need to do."

I HEAR YOU,
THOMAS MERTON

I hear you, Thomas Merton,
in the silence of the woods, in the deep of the hermitage,
your typewriter, old and beaten, functional,
I hear your keys click in the middle of the night,
in the early dew of the morning you loved so dear.

I hear you, Thomas Merton, in your passion
your sorrow and head shaking against the wars that raged,
the war in Vietnam and the war in your soul,
the longing for peace and the peace you found that could not be understood
by those who love the art of war and live for death.

I hear you, Thomas Merton, sitting in the afternoon
watching the sun descend beyond the woods of your hermitage,
observing every little leaf and flower in joy,
happy to find deer and bear as your companions.

I hear you, Thomas Merton, in every word you wrote,
for in the beginning was the Word –

and then there were words and words and words.

MUSINGS OF A POTENTIAL MONK

"What is this?" I asked,
He turned to me and with a smile
replied, "It's just for you, it's special,
I've been working on it for quite a while.
I think with time you will find it light
though most believe it out of style."

He placed His carpenter's tools aside,
and brushed some wood chips from His hair.
"Pick it up and see how it feels" he offered,
and pointed to a dusty corner where
a great Cross lay upon it's side.
All I could do was stand and stare.

It was this Cross of which I'd heard
of which I'd known for fearful years,
and turned away to vain pursuits
to ignore this summit of all my fears.
Yet now face to face with hideous beauty,
which beckoned to a life of tears.

"Don't be afraid," he gently said,
"I bore one heavier than that, you know."
A step forward, intrigued, for it seemed
to beckon and call to me just so,
as if some quiet Spirit there was,
would urge me pick it up and go.

Such loving workmanship, yet cruel to touch
How could I not respond to that call
Borne teasingly upon my shoulders,
but so heavy I felt sure I must fall,
"Will you take it up and walk with me,
if so, it shall weigh but naught at all."

In fear a faltering first step I took
To try the weight – could I be one more
who in his Master's footsteps could walk
to embrace this death as Heaven's door
And death it was, yet true life, I sensed
in a way I had never known before.

With no word to Him I grasped the Cross,
and sudden upon my shoulders it laid
But heavily I crashed unto the ground
and lay there sobbing and afraid.
"Wait," He gently said, "You cannot alone
bear such weight without my aide."

With eyes of tender love He bent
stooping to help me from the ground.
"My burden is easy, my Cross is light,
yours too heavy, as you have found.
But with me lift, and we shall walk,
and in a new life you shall abound.

"So many their Cross flee in fear,
afraid they cannot bear the pain.
But if only they would ask My help,
They would find in loss great gain,
for in each Cross I meet the soul,
to bring My presence in its pain."

First trembling step, and then another,
but lo! lighter the Cross seemed now to be.
And instead of wearisome to shoulder,
in joy my heart leaped, singing free
Exultant I cried out to the heavens
"I once was blind, but now I see!".

Now this very Cross from which I ran,
has lifted me higher towards His throne.
That death I feared was truly life,
the reality of His love completely shown
For as He promised to all who come,
no one carries his cross alone.*

 * **March 2008 Great Lent at Holy Trinity Monastery Butler PA**

Made in the USA
Middletown, DE
12 April 2022

63853710R00106